GUIDE TO PSYCHIC POWER

GUIDE TO PSYCHIC POWER

Rosemary Ellen Guiley

Visionary Living, Inc.
New Milford, Connecticut

Guide to Psychic Power

By Rosemary Ellen Guiley

© Copyright Visionary Living, Inc., 2015
All rights reserved.

No part of this book may be reproduced in any form or used without permission.

Front cover design: April Slaughter
Back jacket and interior design by Leslie McAllister

ISBN: 978-0-9860778-8-3 (pbk.)
ISBN: 978-0-9860778-9-0 (e-pub)

Published by Visionary Living, Inc.
New Milford, Connecticut
www.visionaryliving.com

Other books by Rosemary Ellen Guiley available from Visionary Living

Dreamwork for Visionary Living
Dream Messages from the Afterlife
Pocket Dream Guide and Dictionary
Develop Your Miracle Mind Consciousness
Calling Upon Angels: How Angels Help Us in Daily Life
Angel Magic for Love and Relationships
Christmas Angels: True Stories of Hope and Healing
Soul Journeys: Past and Future Lives
Haunted by the Things You Love
The Djinn Connection
The Art of Black Mirror Scrying
Guide to the Dark Side of the Paranormal
Ouija Gone Wild

Table of Contents

Introduction — xi

Part I: Your Psychic Power

1. Psychic Power is Your Birthright — 1
2. Your Psychic Power and Auric Blueprint — 7
3. Psychic Speak — 15
4. Opening Your Psychic Gate — 33
5. Cosmic Connections — 45
6. The Holistic Psychic Lifestyle — 55

Part II: Keys for Developing Your Psychic Power

Introduction to the Keys — 69

Key #1: Psychic Power Breathing — 71

Key #2: Meditation Adventures — 77

Key #3: Chakra Energizing — 87

Key #4: Ball of Light — 91

Key #5: Expanded Vision — 95

Key #6: Expanded Listening — 101

Key #7: Riding the Waves	105
Key #8: Remote Viewing	107
Key #9: Reading Objects and Photographs	113
Key #10: Reading Auras	119
Key #11: Dowsing with a Pendulum	121
Key #12: The Dream Oracle	127
Key #13: Yes or No	133
Key #14: Card Games	139
Key #15: The Open Book	149
Key #16: Future News	151
Key #17: Hide and Seek	155
Key #18: Messages in Voices	159
Key #19: Colored Dots	163
Key #20: Shapes and Symbols	167
Key #21: Mirror Images	169
Key #22: The Lotus Eye	173

Part III: Using Your Psychic Power

7. Practical Psychic Power	179
8. Getting the Message	181

9. Problem Solving and Decision Making	187
10. Finding Your Purpose and Achieving Goals	191
11. Increasing Your Prosperity	197
12. Improving Your Relationships	203
13. Enhancing Your Creativity, Health and Self-Improvement	209
14. Achieving Abundant Living	221
Appendix: Psychic Etiquette	227
About the Author	233
Bibliography	235

Introduction

Everyone is born with an innate psychic ability that serves as a rich source of guidance, wisdom, insight, creativity, and healing. Psychic ability enhances everything we do—our jobs, relationships, self-esteem, creativity, health—and our ability to dream bold visions of the future. Some people are able to use this ability easily and naturally, while others need to rediscover it. Regardless of your ability, you can enhance your skill through self-training and practice.

You will benefit from this book if:

You *need new direction in life.* All of us go through periods in which we feel overwhelmed by problems, or we're being pulled in too many directions, or we can't seem to get a clear head about making decisions. You can take control of your life now by putting your psychic power to work for you.

You want to improve your performance at work. Whether you are self-employed, starting up a new business, or working for a company or organization, you can shine with ideas, visionary thinking, and creative problem-solving. The psychic skill-building exercises in this book will show you how.

You have a hard time making up your mind. You struggle with decisions, engaging in vacillation, weighing of pros and cons, and fence-sitting. Once decisions are made, you then engage in endless second-guessing. Stop! Your psychic sense will help you see things more clearly. You can make sound decisions more quickly, and free up time and energy to move ahead.

Things often seem to go wrong for you. And you find yourself singing the same glum refrains, such as "The story of my life!" or "This always happens to me." You will change those refrains to a happier tune when you learn to understand and trust the guidance of your psychic power.

You want to be more creative. Do you feel that you're not using your full potential, but you're not sure what to do about it? There is tremendous creativity within all of us. You don't necessarily need to drop what you're doing and take up something radically new. Your psychic power will show you how to unfold like a blossoming flower.

Things are going well but you'd like them to go even better. Our psychic power is constantly guiding us toward achieving our highest fulfillment in terms of abundance, success, satisfaction, love, health, and spiritual development.

You picked up this book. Your psychic sense guided here. The message from your Higher Self is, "I can help you find what you need. I want to help you."

So start now. You'll find the ninety-five exercises in this book easy to do. I know from my own experience that if self-improvement exercises are too complicated, they don't get done. The exercises here are simple, solid, basic, proven, and very effective. Some will be familiar to you, others will be new. Try them all. They are designed to acquaint you with the various nuances of your psychic power and help you to gain confidence in the information you receive. Everyone experiences the psychic faculty in his or her own unique way. The exercises in this book will help you develop your own personal style.

Part III of this book, "Using Your Psychic Power," will show you practical ways to put your skill to work in the areas of self-improvement, relationships, work, creativity, prosperity, health, and visionary thinking.

A more abundant and satisfying life awaits you. Psychic power is one of our best tools for building an abundant and satisfying life. Take what is naturally yours and fulfill your dreams.

– Rosemary Ellen Guiley

Part I
Your Psychic Power

1

Psychic Power Is Your Birthright

Every day, psychic sense saves people from inconvenience, injury, and even death. And it may have even saved the world from nuclear disaster.

In 1983, the world came perilously close to nuclear war. Only a few people knew then how narrowly an exchange of nuclear missiles between the United States and the former Soviet Union was avoided. The story did not reach the public until October 1998, when it was reported by news agencies around the world.

In 1983, tension was high following the shooting down of a Korean Air jumbo jet by the Soviet Union. The Boeing 747 passenger jet had strayed into Soviet air space and been shot down by the military, killing everyone on board.

On the night of September 1983, a Russian army lieutenant colonel and software engineer named Stanislav Petrov was on duty at a military satellite surveillance center near Moscow. The surveillance provided early warning of any incoming missiles. Just after midnight, Petrov's computer screen suddenly flashed the words, MISSILE ATTACK. A piercing alarm sounded. The system indicated that a missile had been launched from a U.S. base.

Petrov's orders were to immediately notify superiors. If missiles were en route, a counterattack would be launched right away. Every second counted.

Stunned, Petrov hesitated, weighing the terrible consequences of confirming an attack. He then noticed that ground-based radar did not indicate missiles had been launched. Within minutes, he concluded that the satellite system had given a false alarm.

But new alarms sounds, indicating four more missiles had been launched from the U.S. base. What if he were wrong? Petrov held firm to his conclusion. It was in part, he said later, a "gut feeling" that no one really wanted to start a nuclear war.

Petrov reported the alarm as false. A subsequent investigation revealed that sunlight reflecting off clouds had been the culprit.

"Petrov's decision to disobey procedure was intuitive," stated the BBC in its 1998 report about the incident.

The story illustrates how the psychic sense or intuition often works: it grabbed Petrov with a visceral "gut feeling" and ran counter to the prevailing data. As a result, a devastating mistake was avoided.

Psychic sense also played a role in one of the most famous disasters of history: the sinking of the luxury liner *Titanic*. Psychic power did not avert the disaster, but it did save lives.

A few days before the *Titanic* was scheduled to depart Southampton, England on its maiden voyage to New York in April 1912, American business magnate J. Pierpont Morgan suddenly canceled his first-class ticket, deciding that it was better for him not to go. He was not alone. Other passengers canceled their tickets, too. Some experienced uneasy dreams about the ship sinking. Some decided it wasn't a good idea to travel, without knowing exactly why. Some were diverted by unexpected events that conflicted with their plans for their trip.

Some inadvertently lost their chance to sail. A group of twenty-two stokers found themselves running late in getting to the dock. They raced up to the ship, but the irate captain told them the ship was going to leave without them. It did, leaving them puzzled and upset over losing their jobs. Days later, their distress turned to profound shock and relief when news came that the *Titanic* had struck an iceberg and sunk. Killed were 1502 of the 2207 passengers aboard. It was one of the worst maritime disasters of peacetime.

The disaster of the *Titanic* would have been much worse if the ship had carried a full load of passengers. In fact, it sailed with only 58 percent of its passenger capacity. Why did the most prestigious and heavily promoted ocean liner of its day attract such a small crowd of passengers? Why was it not fully booked on its highly touted grand maiden voyage? And why did some people not follow through on their plans to sail?

The answer is psychic sense. You can also call it premonition, precognition, psychic foresight, hunch, gut instinct, or intuition, but they are all terms describing the same faculty: the ability to know something that cannot be explained by the facts at hand. For some people who planned to travel on the *Titanic*, their psychic sense spoke clearly: they had nightmarish dreams about the ship sinking that seemed very realistic, or they had profound unease about going. For others, the psychic sense was more indirect: there was no inkling of disaster, but they felt strongly guided by some inner voice or prompting to change their plans. And for others, events of the world in the form of synchronicity intervened: unexpected conflicts of time, such as happened to the group of stokers who were "inexplicably" tardy for the big day.

There have been many cases of psychic guidance that have prevented people from being injured or losing their lives in accidents and disasters. We hear about them every day in the news: "Something just told me not to get on the plane," or "I decided not to take the same route to work, so I was late and that meant I missed being in the bomb blast," or "I decided to leave earlier than I'd planned, so I missed the accident that tied up the freeway for two hours," and so on. A study done some years ago of passenger loads on American trains which had accidents showed a remarkable drop-off in average numbers of passengers on the days of the accidents. Conclusion: *something* prompted people to alter their plans or miss the trains.

That "something" is psychic power.

Psychic power works for us in more than diverting disaster. Most of us, hopefully, will never face such dire circumstances as described above. Yet our psychic power still works for us all the time, pushing us, pulling us, guiding us, encouraging us, and warning us about everything—yes, *everything*—that goes on in our lives. Psychic power is behind the impulse to call someone, the inspiration to try something novel, the decision to take a risk, the solution to a problem, the right words to say and the seemingly impulsive act to take. Psychic power works for us on the big things and the small things in life.

In preparation for a trip to Japan, I bought some gifts for the people I would be seeing there. Gift-giving is an important social custom in Japan. I purchased three angel music boxes for three women I had met on a previous trip there, and whom I would be meeting together again on this trip. Each music box was slightly different. One had a pink angel playing a harp. One had a blue angel playing a trumpet. And one had an angel taking the hand of a child. Each played a different melody. Did it matter which one I gave to which person? I didn't know any of the women well, yet I had strong impressions as to which music box should go to which person. I wrapped the angels up and put the recipients' names on them.

When the gifts were opened, it turned out that each woman had the "right" angel. The lady whose favorite color was pink received the pink angel. The lady whose favorite color was blue received the blue angel. The song played by the angel with a child was a favorite of the lady who received that music box. They were pleased and surprised at how personal their gifts were. How had I known those things, they wanted to know. I smiled and said, "I think the angels told me."

How did it work out that way? Was I just lucky when I decided who would get which angel?

I let my psychic power choose for me. As I held each angel, I allowed myself to "feel" the name that went with it.

My psychic power has worked for me in countless ways, making decisions major and minor. I have learned through trial and error that if I override psychic sense, things invariably don't work out the way I anticipated. We've all been in the same position, when we've found ourselves saying, "I *knew* I should/shouldn't have..."

Most people do not regard themselves as psychic, even though everyone is born with that faculty. Thus, they unwittingly shut themselves off from a tremendous source of guidance, wisdom, insight, creativity, and healing. When you discover how keenly psychic you really are, a whole new dimension of living is revealed. Psychic power enhances every aspect of life—our jobs, relationships, self-esteem, creativity, health, and our ability to dream bold visions of the future. When we allow our natural psychic power to work for us, we are better equipped to make good decisions, for everything from driving a particular route to making career changes to investing our money to involvements with other people. We are more likely to have great ideas and know how to act on them, and feel more energized and full of vitality.

All of us can reach within and find this gift and develop it. What's more, it is easier to do than you might think. The exercises in this book will show you how.

Self Test

In this self test, check all that you feel apply to you:

- You have hunches or gut feelings about how something will work out
- You are prompted by your good judgment
- You get lucky breaks
- You inexplicably know something
- You have a feeling that something will happen
- Your dreams give you guidance
- You frequently find yourself in the right place at the right time
- Your guesses turn out to be uncannily accurate
- You feel guided by higher powers
- You have flashes of insight in which things seem crystal clear
- You feel strong impulses to do something that runs contrary to reason

If you answered yes to even one statement, then you've affirmed your basic, inborn ability to be psychic. That ability may not be readily apparent to you now, but with a little encouragement it can become a strong and powerful force in your life. You are psychic *and* smart if you *act* on any of the above.

How can psychic power help you in your life? Count the ways:

- Plan your day more effectively to make the best use of your time
- Make decisions big and small without fence-sitting, vacillating and second-guessing
- Sense the moods and feelings of others so you can make appropriate responses
- Sense the best timing and approach for relating to others, such as asking for favors, mending strained relationships and improving personal communications
- Motivate others
- Handle confrontations in an effective manner
- Improve your health and the health of others
- Find lost objects
- Feel more comfortable about risk-taking
- Stimulate more creativity, energy, and vitality
- Improve your self-confidence and self-image

You can enjoy all these benefits and more by letting your psychic power be your guide.

2

Your Psychic Power and Auric Blueprint

Is there a difference between being intuitive and being psychic? Is it possible to be one without the other?

The two are different terms for the same faculty.

The term "psychic" comes from the Greek word *psyche*, which means "of the soul." It refers to our inner state of being. Psychic ability thus springs from the very core of our being. It truly is a gift—a gift from the Creator, the Source of All Being, a resource to help us realize our full potential as human beings and as souls.

Psychic power involves a knowing that comes from beyond the five senses, yet makes use of the senses in order to convey information. It functions in a variety of ways that overlap with each other. Here are descriptions:

Precognition

Precognition is direct knowledge or perception of the future, obtained through extraordinary means. Precognition is the most frequently reported of all psychic power experiences. According to studies, it occurs most often (60 to 70 percent) in dreams. Precognition also occurs in waking visions, sudden thoughts, and the inner voice. Most experiences of precognition happen within one to two days of an event. Some can occur months, even years, before the actual event takes place.

Everyone has at least one experience of precognition during life. Such episodes may involve traumatic events. The emotional intensity surrounding trauma seems to break through the normal barriers most of us have to accessing information from the future or distant places.

We also experience lesser precognitions that involve daily affairs. For example, you may have a sudden and certain feeling that you will encounter a particular person, whom you have not seen in a long time, later in the day. You shrug it off as imagination—and then run into that very person.

Precognition is the basis for divination, prophecy, and prediction, which have been practiced by all societies around the world since ancient times. Traditionally, individuals with natural exceptional psychic gifts, or who had been specially trained, served in official capacities to advise heads of state about the future. To stimulate precognition, they induced trance or read the random patterns of nature, such as clouds, the flights of birds or rising smoke, or tossed objects, such as stones or bones. These methods and tools do not in themselves contain precognitive information, but are a means to open the psychic faculty.

Premonition

Premonition is a first cousin to precognition, and is usually experienced as a foreboding or warning. Premonitions are often vague and more generalized, such as a "feeling" that something unpleasant may happen. Premonitions probably were behind many of the canceled plans to sail on the *Titanic*.

Telepathy

Telepathy is mind-to-mind communication of thoughts, feelings, ideas, sensations, and mental images. Telepathy can occur between any two persons, or even among a group of persons. The greater the emotional bond between persons, the more likely they will experience telepathy naturally. You have probably had experiences where you have thought the same thought, even the same words, almost simultaneously with another person.

Clairvoyance

Clairvoyance is "clear-seeing." It involves images and visions of distant or inaccessible people, places, and objects with both inner and outer sight. Information or knowledge may arise spontaneously with the visions. Clairvoyance is a term that has been supplanted by more modern ones, such as "medical intuition" to describe the ability to see into the body and its energy field to detect imbalances and disease, and "remote viewing" to describe seeing things at a distance.

Clairaudience

Clairaudience is "clear hearing." You hear information through an inner voice or through a direct, disembodied voice that seems to originate in the space around you as though an invisible person were speaking to you.

For example, Sandy was getting ready to leave for the store when she heard a distinct inner voice say, "Don't go to the store." She immediately thought that this was silly, that there was no reason for her not to go. But strangely, she felt compelled to follow the voice's instructions, and so she postponed her plans. She later heard on the news that a gas main had exploded in front of the store at about the time she would have been there. Dozens of people were seriously injured.

Clairaudience also involves other sounds, such as music.

Clairsentience

Clairsentience is "clear sensing," and describes a range of physical sensations that convey information, such as smells, tastes, tactile perceptions, and body reactions such as tightness in the belly, tingling of the skin, and so on. For example, your psychic faculty tells you something is wrong whenever you experience a certain heaviness in your abdomen.

Psychokinesis

Psychokinesis (PK) is the influence of mind over matter. Parapsychology research has established that we can alter the physical environment with our thought or will. In studies, subjects have altered the toss of dice, changed temperatures in rooms, and changed the properties of water, among other experiments. Healing at a distance is a form of PK, as is weather control performed by shamans.

The Auric Field

You will understand your own psychic power, and be able to develop it more quickly, if you are familiar with your auric field, which is your energy blueprint. The aura is an envelope of vital energy that radiates from everything in nature: minerals, plants, animals, and humans. The aura is not visible to normal vision, but can be perceived through the psychic senses. It may be seen as a multi-colored mist that fades off into space with no definite boundary, and containing sparks, rays and streamers. It may be felt as a textured substance, or even experienced as a collection of emotions or smells.

The existence of the aura has been known since ancient times. Descriptions of it appeared in the writings and art of Egypt, India, Greece, and Rome, among other civilizations. In the sixteenth century, Paracelsus was one of the first Western scholars to expound upon the astral body, which he described as a "fiery globe." In the eighteenth century, the clairvoyant Emanuel Swedenborg said in his *Spiritual Diary* that "there is a spiritual sphere surrounding every one, as well as a natural and corporal one."

Scientific study of the aura began in the late eighteenth century, when Franz Anton Mesmer put forth the theory of "animal magnetism," an electro-magnetic force that could be transmitted from one person to another via the hands and eye gazing, and thus could effect healing. In 1845, Baron Karl von Reichenbach, a German chemist, announced the discovery of the "odic force" energy. Reichenbach's clairvoyant test subjects sat in darkened rooms and saw flame-like energy radiating from finger tips, animals, plants, magnets, and crystals. The subjects described phenomena such as seeing flames of red, orange, green, and violet, which alternately appeared and disappeared; a violet red that disappeared in a smoke-like vapor; and intermingled sparks and stars among all colors.

Shortly before World War I, Dr. Walter J. Kilner, who was in charge of electro-therapy at St. Thomas's Hospital in London, discovered that the human aura could be made visible if viewed through an apparatus containing a coal-tar dye called dicyanin, which made ultraviolet light visible. Kilner saw the aura as a faint haze that sometimes could be separated into two or three portions. It enveloped the whole body.

While scientific measurement of the aura remains elusive today, anyone who trains to become an energy healer knows the aura exists and learns how to perceive it and work with it.

In the early 1980s, I began studying energy healing, learning a variety of techniques. The basic principle behind energy healing is that the healer is a channel for the universal life force, which carries the power to heal. The universal life force is a substance that permeates everything in existence and is essential to life and health. It is known by various names, including *chi, ki, prana* and *mana*. When we are full of the universal life force, we are healthy and vital. If we lack in it, we become ill. According to energy medicine, problems manifest first in the outer layers of the aura and then affect the body. Healers use their psychic power to perceive problem areas in the aura and body, and then channel the universal life force to the affected areas through their hands.

In energy healing training, I learned how to feel and see the aura, and receive impressions related to another person's well-being. I learned how to clear and smooth blockages in the aura, which can alleviate physical symptoms and emotional distress.

The aura has several envelopes, or layers, to it. Various names are applied to them. Some esoteric traditions split the aura into as many as five or seven bodies. There are four primary bodies, or layers, that are most relevant to developing psychic power: etheric, emotional, mental, and astral.

Etheric body

Immediately next to the physical body is the etheric body, which is an energy double of the physical. Many energy healers work in the etheric body, where they see symptoms of illness that have not yet manifested physically.

Emotional body

Next to the etheric body is the emotional body. This is the part of our energy field that retains impressions from our emotions. Many sources of illness can be detected here. Long-time emotional imbalances contribute to physical illness. For me, this is the layer of the aura that I see first. I "see" such things as emotional wounds, repressed emotions, and emotional difficulties. These impressions are conveyed to me in images, many of which are symbolic like dream images; in words that arise inside my mind; and in the holistic, psychic sense of "knowing."

Mental body

Next to the emotional body is the mental body, the plane of thoughts. In all mystical and esoteric traditions, thought creates reality. We become what we think. First we think it, then we say and do it. If you think you are a failure, you will create a reality of failure around you. If you think you are a success, you will create that reality instead.

All of us deal with programming from our upbringing and experiences that affect us throughout life. Negative programming needs to be altered if we are to achieve our fullest potential. All of us have the ability to change in significant ways if we make the choice to do so, and act on that choice.

Astral body

Beyond the mental body is the astral body. This outer layer extends into space. It concerns our spiritual side—the soul part of us that is evolving through life. The Higher Self resides in this outer layer.

Psychic impressions of the aura are subjective. Each person sees or feels the aura according to his or her own psychic impressions. Later on in this book, you will learn how to psychically read an aura, and how to move energy through your own auric field.

Chakras

The universal life force enters the aura and body through centers called chakras, a Sanskrit terms meaning "wheels." Chakras are called wheels because they are shaped like multi-colored lotus petals or spoked wheels which rotate at various speeds as they process the universal life force. The chakras act as transformers, taking the universal life force and distributing it throughout the layers of the aura and the body. If the chakras become sluggish or blocked, health is affected.

There are seven major chakras and hundreds of minor ones. The seven major chakras, which are most directly concerned with physical health, lie along the spinal column and the head, from the base of the spine to the top of the head. Each chakra is associated with a major endocrine gland, a major nerve plexus, a physiological function and a psychic function. Each chakra also has its own unique number of spokes in its wheel. The higher the position along the spinal column, the more complex the chakra, the greater the number of spokes, and the higher the functions.

Each chakra has its own color associated with it as well. When the chakras are balanced and healthy, their colors are clear and luminous, and their rotation is smooth. In poor health, they become cloudy and irregular or sluggish in rotation. Chakras that are blocked adversely influence the body functions they govern. In alternative healing, there are techniques for clearing chakra blockages and stimulating rotation.

The seven major chakras are:

- *The root,* located at the base of the spine. It is concerned with self-preservation; connection to family, country and race; connection to the physical world; animal nature; and taste and smell. It is red in color.

- *The spleen,* which lies near the genitals. It governs sexuality and reproduction; personal power; and ambition. It is orange-red.

- *The solar plexus,* which rests just above the navel. It is associated with the emotions, gut instinct and the intuition. It affects the adrenals, pancreas, liver and stomach. It is yellow.

- *The heart,* which is located midway between the shoulder blades in the center of the chest. It governs the thymus gland and influences immunity to disease. It is linked to higher consciousness and unconditional love. It is green.

- *The throat,* located at the base of the throat. It is associated with creativity and self-expression, and the search for Truth. It also influences the thyroid and parathyroid glands, and metabolism, and is associated with certain states of expanded consciousness. It is silvery blue.

- *The brow,* located on the forehead between and slightly above the brows. It is called the third eye for its influence over spiritual enlightenment. It is associated with the pituitary gland, the pineal gland, intelligence, intuition and psychic powers. It is indigo.

- *The crown,* located just above the top of the head. It is not associated with any glands, but reveals the individual's level of conscious evolution. It cannot be activated until all the other chakras are refined and balanced; when it is, it brings supreme enlightenment and cosmic consciousness. It is violet.

In the Key exercises in Part II, you will learn more how to work with the chakras to activate your psychic power.

Kundalini

The chakras are home to a psycho-spiritual energy, called kundalini. Kundalini is Sanskrit for "she who is coiled," named for divine female creative energy which lies coiled like a serpent in the root chakra. Kundalini slumbers away within us until it is activated by spiritual awakening or creativity. Developing psychic power also awakens kundalini, which opens higher powers within us.

The phenomena associated with kundalini vary, and include strange physical sensations and movements, pain, clairaudience, visions, brilliant lights, super lucidity, psychical powers, ecstasy, bliss, and transcendence of self. Kundalini has been described as liquid fire and liquid light that pours through the body. A common experience of kundalini is a sensation of heat or tingling that begins at the base of the spine and travels up the body.

Kundalini experiences are described in spiritual traditions around the world since ancient times. It is a universal phenomenon. When we awaken our higher centers of consciousness, we are filled with a new energy that brings heightened creativity and psychic power.

Sometimes psychic power is accompanied by sensations of heat, tingling, electricity coursing through the body, and buzzing or ringing in the ears. These phenomena also are linked to kundalini.

3

Psychic Speak

The psychic faculty has four primary avenues for conveying information to us:

- Body
- Mind
- Emotions
- Spirit

The Body

Psychic power can make use of all of your physical senses to register itself for attention. The most common of these sensory experiences are:

Physical feelings in the body
Strong body sensations are the most frequently reported phenomena in psychic functioning. Examples are a tingling of skin,

warmth, coldness, a peculiar sensation in the gut, tickling, and so on. Beethoven said his whole body shivered and his hair stood on end when inspiration struck. He felt plunged into a mysterious state of oneness with the world, in which all the forces of nature were his instruments. Most of the time, our physical psychic cues are not so intense in a mystical sense, but they do help to steer us in making decisions.

Jennifer was interviewing candidates for a job. She needed someone who could hit the deck running and would be reliable for meeting the tight deadlines coming up. The opening had drawn a large number of applicants, many of whom looked promising. Jennifer had interviewed many persons when she received an application from a woman whose resume looked great. She had all of the qualifications and more for the job. She had good references. Her background made her an ideal addition to the company for the long-term picture. Jennifer scheduled an appointment for an interview, and looked forward to meeting her. Maybe her search would come to an end.

When the woman walked into her office, Jennifer had an immediate, visceral reaction: she felt as though she had been punched in the abdomen. It was strong and took her by surprise. At first she thought she was having a reaction to something she had eaten for lunch. Then she realized that it was more like an anxiety. She strove to disregard it and carried on with the interview.

The applicant was pleasant and eager for the job. She gave the rights answers to all of Jennifer's questions. She could start right away. The feeling in Jennifer's abdomen spread throughout her like a malaise. She began to feel as though she were in two separate worlds: talking to the job applicant and trying to analyze her own unease.

Jennifer thanked the woman and said she would be in touch.

Jennifer was puzzled. Why had she reacted so strongly to the woman? She reviewed the application. Everything looked terrific on paper. The interview itself had gone well. The next step would be to check the references and previous employment. But whenever Jennifer thought about hiring the woman, she felt a tightening in her gut. It seemed like a warning. Something was not right.

Jennifer decided not to pursue hiring the woman. She continued her search and found another candidate whose stated qualifications were good, though not as good as the other woman's. When Jennifer interviewed that candidate, she experienced a warm, buoyant feeling, and a lightness in her abdomen. Everything professional checked out, and the person was hired.

Much later, Jennifer learned that the woman who had seemed like the ideal candidate was in fact much the opposite. She had a history of troubles on the job. It validated Jennifer's gut-level warning. The person who was hired, meanwhile, performed better than might have been expected.

Jennifer experienced a psychic power warning through strong body sensations. Her gut instinct gave her information not available to the rational mind.

Visions

Psychic sight can give us the big and clear picture and the clear picture. Images are powerful conveyors of information, much better than words. Most often, visual images play out on the inner eye. For example, let's say you are struggling to come up with attractive packaging for a new product. Design after design goes in the waste bin. Suddenly, you get a flash of what the packaging should look like, seeing it very clearly. In another example, you may get a picture of what may happen in the future, such as the chart of a stock that you are interested in buying.

Sometimes images need to be interpreted, just like dreams. I receive visual impressions when I do readings for others. Some images are straightforward, others are not. In one case, I saw a piece of cauliflower over a man's throat chakra. I said to myself, "What does cauliflower have to do with the throat chakra?" A soon as I asked myself the question, the answer arose spontaneously within. In the blink of an eye, I understood that the man's self-expression was rather like a piece of cauliflower—bland. He confirmed that he indeed was struggling with expressing himself in a bolder and more assertive way.

The images that your psychic power delivers to you will always be appropriate for your own unique Psychic Speak.

Psychic power also uses images to represent yes or no, such as a green light and a red light. These images may arise spontaneously, or we can train our psychic faculty to use certain key images and symbols.

Sounds and voices

Perhaps your psychic faculty gives you a ringing or buzzing in the ears, or voices. "Whenever my intuition gives me a positive sign, I always hear bells ringing," a man told me at one of my workshops. "They sound like cathedral bells rung in celebration. Sometimes the sound is so distinct that I think there are bells somewhere actually ringing." A woman told me that she, too, heard sounds she associated with her psychic power, especially rushing water that sounded like a huge waterfall.

It is not uncommon to hear inner voices say "yes," "no,: "forget it," "you have it," "don't worry," or offer specific instructions or advice such as, "Take the next train." Such voices usually seem to come from within, and can be quite commanding.

Voices also may seem to emanate from the space around you. Throughout history, such voices have often been attributed to otherworldly sources, such as angels, spirit guides, the dead, saints, and even God. In ancient times, one could not be considered a prophet unless one had auditory experiences that evidenced direct communication with the divine.

Hearing voices is a phenomenon called "audition." Audition occurs in waking consciousness and in meditative, contemplative, or distracted states that border on sleep. Audition also occurs in dreams.

Paula, a teacher, told me, "When I ask my intuition for guidance, I often get an answer in a clear voice that seems to come from just above my shoulders. At first I thought it was a person speaking. Then I thought I was imagining things. But I have learned that the voice is right, so I pay attention. It usually happens when I'm not concentrating about whatever I'm seeking guidance on."

Tastes

Yes, psychic power can use our taste buds to prod us in the right direction. Good tastes, bad tastes, dry mouth, stinging mouth, and moist mouth all can be signals of yes or no. Some people experience particular tastes that are associated with personal pleasant or unpleasant situations. "When something isn't right but not in an obvious sort of way, I'll often get a taste of iron in my mouth," a workshop participant told me. "I don't know where it comes from. But I've learned over time that it happens whenever I should be careful, that something doesn't look as good as it seems to be."

Synesthesia

Some people experience their intuition in an odd blending of senses, such as hearing colors or tasting shapes. This blending of senses is called "synesthesia," which comes from the Greek terms meaning "feeling together." A minority of the population experiences synesthesia as their norm all the time. Most synesthetes, as they are called, experience only one or two crossed connections; not all five senses are blended. The most common crossed connection is colored hearing, in which certain sounds produce lines, spheres, or other geometric colored shapes that appear in the person's near field of vision.

Although few people have synesthesia, researchers have hypothesized that the capability for it may have been part of our ancient and original blueprint. It may be closely allied to our so-called primitive instincts, which makes it a potential first cousin to psychic power. In the future, the ability to experience blended senses may be more the norm than the exception.

Exercise for the senses

Everyone processes information through their senses in a different way. Typically, we have a dominant sense that registers the strongest impressions. Try this exercise to find out more about how your senses give you information:

> *Close your eyes, breathe deeply and relax. Clear your mind of its busy thoughts. With each breath, feel yourself loosening up and expanding.*
>
> *Now imagine that you are in a beautiful forest, walking along a path. Look up at the trees... notice how green they are... the shapes of their trunks, branches and leaves... Look at the brush and flowers alongside the path... Notice the kinds of blossoms and the colors... See the sky painted across the background...*
>
> *Feel the firmness of the path beneath your feet... the indentations in the ground... stones and pebbles... Stop and touch a group of flowers... feel the texture of the stems, the velvet of the blossoms... Touch the trees and feel their leaves...*

A breeze blows gently... it brings strange smells... identify the smells... hear the breeze in the trees...

Insects buzz in the air... small creatures rustle in the leaves... your feet make soft noises on the path... Still yourself and listen for more subtle sounds...

You come to a house... a picnic table has been set up outside the house... on it is a freshly baked cherry pie... You sit down and eat a piece of pie and drink a beverage... You savor each bite and swallow...

When you are finished eating, return your consciousness to the room. Breathe deeply, pushing the breath down through the soles of your feet. Open your eyes.

Make notes about your sensory experience. Which sense was strongest and most vivid for you? Perhaps you had two senses that were equally vivid. These are the senses most likely to convey psychict impressions to you.

Emotions

Body sensations related to psychic power may be commonplace, but for many of us, the psychic faculty speaks loudest through the emotions: good feelings, bad feelings, sad feelings, joy, elation, depression, dread—the entire range of human emotional expression.

Most of us have had at least one experience of psychic power that manifested as inexplicable dread: we were about to do or undertake something, and an inexplicable dread took hold of us so that we changed our minds and actions accordingly.

Inexplicable and strong feelings also prompt us to do things that defy reason, but which are right. Mona Lisa Schulz, a psychiatrist, neuroscientist, and medical intuitive, describes many of these kinds of experiences in her book *Awakening Intuition: Using Your Mind-Body Network for Insight and Healing*. Once, on one of the first nights that Schulz was on duty as an intern in a hospital emergency room, an elderly woman was brought in after collapsing at home. She seemed to be recovered, but was admitted to stay overnight because no one was at home to care for her.

Although nothing seemed to be obviously wrong with the woman, Schulz experienced something that told her otherwise:

> As I approached her gurney, I began to get a vague, fuzzy, yet insistent feeling that seemed to cut through all the noise and commotion around me. I just had a sudden conviction, seeming to come out of nowhere, that contrary to the physical evidence, all was not right with this patient.
>
> I wanted her to get an EKG. Don't ask me why. Her chart indicated no past history of heart trouble, and the examining physician hadn't noted any signs of cardiac problems.

Schulz prevailed in getting an EKG ordered. Her psychic power next directed her to check medical records. There she found files on the patient documenting a history of heart problems. The EKG showed that she was not fine, but was having a heart attack. Schultz said her own gut instinct had helped to save the woman's life.

Because of its link to emotions, the psychic faculty has long had the stereotype of being a "woman's thing." A woman's intuition usually is described in emotional terms, and something women have and men don't admit to having. (Men are supposedly more rational and logical.) The debate over the merit of emotions versus reason has been going on since ancient times. Plato viewed emotions as a prison and reason as the liberation from that prison. Aristotle countered that emotions have a logic of their own, and have to be understood on their own terms. Our scientific worldview has favored Plato: reason is a higher function than emotion, and knowledge is based on what can be measured and quantified, not felt or experienced. Fortunately, those stereotypes are disappearing as we learn more about how the psychic faculty functions, how it works in conjunction with reason, and how both sexes use it as part of the human arsenal for innovation, success, and even survival in the world.

We are emotional as well as rational beings. Psychic power speaks *through* emotions, and is best able to guide us when we apply all of our thinking and feeling processes.

Emotional psychic power brings great ideas and inspiration as well as direction. Feeling profoundly connected to nature or swept up in a tidal wave of emotion can literally flood us with intuitive light. Asked how he got his ideas for his compositions, Beethoven said many of them came out of his emotions. "They come to me in the silence of the night or in the early morning, stirred into being by moods," he said.

The Mind

Psychic power works on a mental level when we have sudden flashes of insight in which we see solutions to problems and information organized in new ways. Our creativity is fueled and we become visionaries of the future. Mental psychic power results from brain-storming, concentration, and problem-solving efforts. We do an intense amount of left-brain thinking and analysis that lay the groundwork for a psychic breakthrough.

Inspiration

Inspiration—those experiences in which profound insights, information, intuitions, and creativity burst through in crystal clarity—is a form of psychic power. Inspiration is behind all great leaps of creativity, genius, innovation, and invention. It is the proverbial bolt from the blue that enables us to see something in an entirely new light or see the big picture or see the future very clearly. Though very mental in nature, it may be accompanied by physical sensations, such as chills, burning, tingling, electric glows, and fuzzy feelings that something profound is about to happen.

We all experience inspiration, but, like other forms of psychic power, it seems to naturally strike more often to a gifted few. You needn't feel left out of the club. Developing your psychic power will increase the flow of inspiration in all areas of your life. Your psychic power makes you more aware of inspiration and shows you how to use it.

Mental concentration must be balanced with relaxation. This prevents mental burn-out, of course, but also is necessary in order for the inspiration to come through. Great artists and thinkers throughout history have known this. Mozart experienced inspiration during times when he was alone and in "good cheer," such as walking after a good meal or traveling in a carriage. The ideas flowed best and most abundantly, he said, and he heard his compositions all at once and not as successive parts. The music poured into his thoughts in finished form, needing only to be committed to paper.

Inspiration struck hotel entrepreneur Conrad Hilton when he doodled. Einstein went sailing or canoeing to disengage his mind. His breakthrough to the Theory of Relativity came with what he called "the happiest thought of my life," when he was inspired by a daydream vision of a person falling off a roof. He realized that the person was both at rest and in motion simultaneously.

When we're trying to solve a problem or come up with new ideas, we can think and think and think about it and still wind up empty-handed (or empty-headed, as the case may be). We can think too hard, in fact. But if we set the matter aside, the answer is likely to burst forth on us when we are doing something entirely different, such as a pleasurable activity, routine tasks, or even while driving in the car.

When we're in a state of passive receptivity, we're likely to be in an alpha state of consciousness. The brainwaves move from the beta range (active thought and waking consciousness) to the alpha range when we meditate, pray, relax, and doze off. Many inspirations also strike in the borderlands of sleep. In the alpha state, our psychic consciousness has freer range to roam and to make an impact on us. It doesn't have to compete with active thought. Ex-Beatle Paul McCartney once related that he woke up from sleep with the song "Yesterday" in his head. The poet William Wordsworth often awakened with poetry forming in his mind.

People who engage in aerobic activity, such as jogging, also experience an increase in inspiration. Aerobic activity releases a flood of endorphins and chemicals in the brain. This in turn stimulates right-brain kinds of experiences, even of a profound spiritual and mystical nature.

Spirit

Psychic power reaches beyond waking consciousness into the mysterious realms of spirit. Guidance may be given through spiritual beings, dreams, and in the form of synchronicity.

Spiritual cues

Reverend Toni G. Boehm, founder of Awakening Hearts Ministry, calls the psychic/intuitive faculty our "spiritual cues" from God. "Intuition is not just the ability to see the future, but more importantly is the ability to recognize the signals that we are being given in the moment that tell us that we are to do something different," Toni explained to me. "For example, we hear cues like turn left, leave now, call Sue immediately, don't take that job regardless of how lucrative it seems—the messages are infinite in nature.

"When we listen, when we go in a direction we don't understand but feel is right, one of two things—or both—are happening," Toni continued. "One is that something in us is ready to be healed, and the experience for the healing lies in the direction in which we are being led. The other is that someone else is ready to be healed and, on an unconscious soul level, we have said yes to being a catalyst or a participant in the healing."

Divine help

Like Toni, many people see psychic power as a form of guidance from higher powers. The psychic voice or prompting comes from God, Goddess, spirit guides, angels, saints, Jesus, Mary, and other holy figures. The helpful intercession of spiritual beings provides a sense of personal comfort and support. We are secure in the knowledge that greater forces are watching out on our behalf. We feel closer to the Divine, the Great Mystery, because of this personal connection.

The certainty that the guidance comes from, say, angels, may begin with childhood experiences, or develop in the course of spiritual study or after a person has a mystical experience. The source of the guidance is identified by the psychic faculty itself. We "know" the messenger and source of our guidance. The knowing arises spontaneously within us. It is our personal badge of Truth.

Psychotherapist and popular author Wayne W. Dyer recounted psychic help that came as the voice of God in his book *Real Magic: Creating Miracles in Every Day Life*:

> On a vacation trip to Panama City, Florida, my wife was driving the car while my daughter Tracy and her cousin were asleep in the back seat. I was napping after six hours

of driving. Suddenly an overwhelming insistence made me sit up and I could see that the car in front of us was about to have a head-on collision with the car in front of it. My wife could not see over the car ahead of us and was unaware of what we were heading for when the car in front of ours swerved toward the gravel alongside the road to avoid the collision. At the same instant that the car swerved, I grabbed the wheel of our car and moved us onto the gravel and the errant driver suddenly became alert. Another horrible head-on crash was avoided.

What was that intuitive feeling that righted me in that instant? You call it what you want; I know it as God speaking to me.

Knowing Truth

The highest function of psychic power transcends the physical realm and literally brings us a holistic understanding of the universe. In mysticism, psychic power is the means by which to achieve direct and immediate Truth and knowledge of the most intimate secrets of life. The discovery of Truth is a unique spiritual journey for every person. The great Indian mystic Sri Aurobindo described the psychic/intuitive faculty as "a memory of the Truth." You do not discover something unknown through psychic power, but rather discover yourself.

You need not be a yogi or ascetic to have an experience of mystical psychic power. A practice of deep meditation or contemplation can bring psychic flashes that reveal the ineffable nature of the cosmos, the Divine Force, the soul, and the unity of all things. P.D. Ouspensky gave the name "Tertium Organum" to what he called "intuitive logic" or "higher logic," defined as the "logic of infinity, the logic of ecstasy," which he said has existed since time immemorial in great philosophical systems and holds the key to the Mysteries. The formula of this intuitive/psychic logic may be expressed as "A is both A and not A," or "A is All." Ouspensky said Plotinus's treatise, *On Intelligible Beauty*, embodies the fullest expression of this logic. Plotinus said that "every thing contains all things in itself... so that all things are everywhere, and all is all. ... And the splendor there is infinite."

Dreams

Dreams have been used since antiquity for guidance and problem-solving. Our ancestors the world over regarded dreams as a direct line of communication to the gods. Dreams were revered as divine gifts; through them, the gods dispensed wisdom, prophecy and direction.

Historically, the understanding of dreams was the province of specially trained priests or dream professionals. These dream wizards could help others interpret their dreams. They also used dreams to pose questions to the gods. Incubation rituals focused intent upon a question; the answer was expected to be revealed during sleep. The Greeks and Romans especially used dreams for healing. Ailing people would make pilgrimages to special dream temples, where they would incubate dreams for healing. They hoped to be healed in their dreams, or to be given prescriptive information that would aid their healing.

The same truth about the power of dreams still applies today. Dreams tap into the psychic resources of our Higher Self. They also deliver messages of spiritual import to us. Our dreams are a hot line to the Creator. We often talk about the need to "sleep on it" before rendering a final decision. In sleep, our intuition helps us sort through information to arrive at a clear answer. The answer may appear in dreams, or may become clear upon awakening. Today we know that everyone, not just the specially trained, can work effectively with his or her dreams.

I have been interested in dreams for most of my life. I consider them one of my greatest psychic allies. My dreams are a constant source of guidance and creative inspiration. The more I pay attention to them, the more responsive they are.

Sometimes we discover the psychic power of dreams inadvertently. Jan was offered a job in another city. It was an attractive offer in money, responsibility and opportunity. Yet Jan wasn't sure she wanted to uproot herself and move. She argued back and forth with herself, listing pros and cons, unable to arrive at a decision that felt right. She had a limited period of time in which to give an answer to her prospective employer.

After wrestling with it unsuccessfully, Jan said to herself, "I can't think about it anymore tonight. I'll worry about it in the morning."

That night, she had a dream in which she was in a sailboat obscured by fog. She couldn't see where she was going.

"When I woke up, I knew what my decision was," Jan told me. "I knew the job wasn't right for me."

I asked her how she knew that the dream reflected her right choice and not just her state of uncertainty.

"It was the feeling I had when I awakened," she said. "I just *knew* that if I took the job and moved, I would feel lost."

The imagery of the sailboat was appropriate for Jan, who is an avid sailor.

Dreamwork may seem daunting at first because the imagery in dreams seems strange or bizarre. Taken literally, dreams often do not make much sense. Our dreams speak to us in images which are symbols. Learning one's own dream language is surprisingly easy. Merely setting our intention to understand our dreams opens the door to understanding them.

Dream incubation is discussed in Key #12.

Synchronicity

Many times psychic power speaks not from within but from without. It is as though the external world, even the universe itself, organizes just for us. People make offhand remarks that give us the answer we seek. We "just happen" to meet someone who provides a solution, or "just happen" to see a book that tells us what we need to know. These "meaningful coincidences" are episodes of synchronicity. They are no accidents of nature. They are part of the ordering of psychic power, and a divine plan for wholeness and balance. When we are in need, we send out a call to the universe. Perhaps we do it consciously by asking for help and guidance; perhaps we do it unconsciously by floundering in a pool of confused thoughts and emotions, or by having a need to fulfill. We get an answer back that guides us toward wholeness. Sometimes the answer is presented through synchronicity. It may be the best way for us to receive the answer. It may be the best way to get our attention after we have failed to pay attention or failed to follow the inner voice. And, it may be the best way to validate opportunities.

Synchronicity gives us the feeling of a greater force at work, as though our destiny and purpose were being played out as part of a grand cosmic tapestry. It is not just a feeling. It is the Truth.

In her work as an intuitive teacher and counselor, Carol Adrienne has witnessed numerous stories of the amazing impact of synchronicity as a form of psychic guidance: career changes, moves, relationships, creativity, business decisions, and more. "I am convinced more than ever that each of us must be alert for the tiny intuitions and ideas that show us where we need to pay attention, and what we need to develop," Carol said in her book, *The Purpose of Your Life*. "Even when we feel blocked and stagnant—as I certainly have been many times—I believe that we are simply at one particular *stage* of the unfolding life purpose that we came to fulfill."

Carol's own unfoldment as artist, author, numerologist and intuition teacher came through many synchronicities: unexpected meetings with people, unexpected phone calls, nudges from others, and opportunities that suddenly jumped into focus. She was guided to move, guided to return to school, guided to pursue various career moves. She had the courage to follow her guidance even when the obstacles against her success were daunting.

"Synchronicities seem to be external answers to an internal psychic state," Carol said. "For example, perhaps we need some particular information, and unexpectedly we run into someone who provides us with exactly what we needed. Synchronicities are a moment in time when we are united with people or information in a way that cannot be described by a linear explanation. They cause us to stop and think. Another name for them is Providence."

It was through synchronistic providence that Carol became partners with James Redfield, author of the hugely popular novels *The Celestine Prophecy* and *The Tenth Insight: Holding the Vision*. *The Celestine Prophecy*, once the biggest-selling nonfiction book in the world, acquainted readers with the concept that everything that happens in our lives has a deeper meaning. Carol read the book at the urging of others. "Over the years, I have learned to listen when people tell me things, so I went out and bought the book," she said. She began to apply the lessons in the book to her counseling practice. One day, an inner prompting urged her to remark about the book to her agent. That led to her collaboration with Redfield to write the nonfiction guides to his novels, *The Celestine Prophecy: An Experiential Guide* and *The Tenth Insight: Holding the Vision: An Experiential Guide*. Both books were bestsellers, and gave a tremendous boost to Carol's own work.

Some of our most important synchronicities come in the words of other people, as demonstrated in Carol's case. Carol calls it the "people have been telling me" syndrome. If others keep urging you to do or try something, you should pay attention, especially if the remarks are unexpected and come from different persons who do not know each other. I have experienced this syndrome myself, in my own life and in the lives of others.

"People are always telling me I should paint," said Gladys, a participant in one of my workshops. Gladys, however, did not feel she had much artistic talent. She thought that her little drawings and handmade notecards for friends and family did not rank as professional art. She thought that others were "trying to be nice" by urging her to paint professionally.

"Perhaps you should listen," I told her. "Think of it this way: it's not so much your friends urging you to paint, but God speaking to you through your friends."

That made a lot of sense to Gladys, and she pledged that she would take action with lessons.

Months later, I received a phone call from a happy and excited Gladys. She had begun lessons with trepidation that her work would be exposed as ordinary. But her teacher quickly saw her innate talent and helped her to develop it. Gladys surprised herself not only by excelling, but by being caught up in a flow of wonderful energy at her new-found confidence and artistic creativity. "I'm so glad I listened," she said. "It's the best thing that ever happened to me."

A few months later, I received an invitation to her first gallery exhibition.

The concept of synchronicity is not new but has been recognized since ancient times. In Eastern philosophy, it is represented in the idea of Tao, or All, and being "in the flow" with the field of the Tao. When we are in the flow, we are in harmony with everything else, and all goes along well. Western philosophy evolved away from a holistic view toward dualism. Synchronicity does not fit into dualism because it runs contrary to traditional esoteric laws of cause and effect. Today we know from quantum physics that causality only partially explains the workings of the universe. Everything is interrelated without dependence upon time or space.

Carl G. Jung helped to restore the concept of synchronicity for the West. Interestingly, he was inspired by Albert Einstein. Jung and Einstein met several times between 1909 and 1913, when Einstein was a professor in

Zurich. Einstein's work on his theory of relativity inspired Jung to ponder a possible relativity of time as well as space.

No insight emerged for Jung for a decade, however. As he explored the nature of the collective unconscious, he encountered numerous synchronicities he could not explain and which defied the odds of chance by astronomical figures. For example, he noted two incidents which happened to the wife of a patient: upon the deaths of her mother and grandmother, birds gathered outside the windows of the death-chambers. Jung knew that in many mythologies, birds represent the soul and are messengers to the gods. That they would gather at the moment of death, when the soul is believed to ascend to heaven, and not at another random time, constituted synchronicity.

Jung found further inspiration for synchronicity from other sources: the *I Ching*, which was introduced to him by Richard Wilhelm, and the work of physicist Wolfgang Pauli, a Nobel Laureate and associate of Einstein who proved the existence of non-local causality. Jung and Pauli collaborated on writing *The Interpretation and Nature of the Psyche*, of which Jung's essay, *Synchronicity*, forms the second part.

In addition, Jung considered the theory of seriality, developed by Paul Kammerer. According to Kammerer, there is a "principal in nature which acts selectively on form and function to bring similar configurations together in space and time; it correlates by affinity."

Jung said synchronicity can be found in events that do not coincide in time and space as well as in events which do, and which have meaningful psychological connections. Synchronicity links the material world to the psychic realm—the world of paranormal phenomena—and the archetypal realm. In other words, synchronicity acts like a bridge between different worlds of awareness. It serves as a conduit for information to travel from the land of the gods to our waking consciousness.

Sometimes synchronicities must happen repeatedly to get our attention. Gregg Levoy, author of *Callings: Finding and Following an Authentic Life*, recounts a series of unusual synchronicities related to a change in his consciousness. After a coveted job as a journalist did not work out, Levoy felt depressed, lost and embarrassed. One day he drove home from work listening to a song called "Desperado" sung by the Eagles. The lyrics refer to "the queen of hearts." When he got out of his car, Levoy found a queen of hearts playing card lying on the curb. At the time, his spiritual path had not yet opened, and so Levoy filed the incident away as a curiosity.

For several years, Levoy searched for a sense of direction in his life. At various intervals, and always in improbable places, he would find a queen of hearts playing card. One even showed up on a sand dune in Oregon.

The meaning of the synchronicities eventually made itself clear to him:

> I came to understand this rather profound administering of chance as directing me toward something that both my writing and my life needed at that time: more heart, less head; more intuition, less intellect; more confessing, less preaching; more of the inner life, the emotional life, the life of the senses; more listening, more following, more of what Carl Jung referred to as the anima, the force of the feminine in a man's life. The queen, of course, is the *archetype* of femininity—of powerful femininity—and I felt myself being compelled toward this energy by the kind of meaningful coincidence that Jung called synchronicity.

Awareness of synchronicity triggers more synchronicity. The more we believe that events have a spiritual purpose and are not random, the more we are aided by synchronicity.

An argument is made that synchronicity negates free will, that we are at the mercy of whatever tide we ride. I do not at all believe that to be the case. Matter constantly reorganizes itself according to affinities. Through free will in our thoughts, choices and actions, we change what is attracted to us. The more positive and assertive we are, the better we are able to achieve our goals. The more negative we are, the more we hold ourselves back and delay or prevent our success. And if we choose simply to ride the tide—the "whatever tide"—then that's what we get: "whatever." Synchronicity is a reflection of the results of your free will choices.

If you have been riding the "whatever tide," you can stop wasting time and energy now. Use your psychic power to get on the track you want. Synchronicity will provide validation and course corrections.

It Is All Interconnected

As you become better acquainted with your psychic power, you will find that it has no sharply defined medium of communication with you. You may experience a predominance of one kind of medium or another, but most of your psychic hits will overlap the categories described above. Psychic power is not just a body phenomenon or strictly an emotional phenomenon, or a mental phenomenon, or a spiritual one. The inner knowing is a combination of all of those things—you cannot separate one from the other.

4

Opening Your Psychic Gate

Psychic power gives you the ability to see and understand your circumstances clearly. It enables you to cut through the murk of uncertainty and doubt. It clears obstructions in your path. Once you allow your psychic power to function freely, everything around you will snap into a different focus.

That does not mean, however, that you will be bombarded constantly by unwanted input. You will naturally learn how to open up and how to close down, how to focus and how to filter.

Use these guidelines to open your psychic gate. They will augment the skill-building exercise in Part II and the practical application exercises in Part III.

Set your intention to be psychic

The intention you set will acknowledge your psychic ability. If you haven't felt psychic in the past, it is because you have ignored or denied your innate ability. Successful people are not successful because they are convinced they are failures. They are successful because they see themselves that way.

Shifting your attitude about your psychic power will open an amazing gate, and insights will come tumbling out.

At the start of every day, resolve that you will be psychic, and that your psychic power will serve you in all ways.

Use affirmations

One effective way to set your intention is through affirmations. Affirmations are positive statements that discipline the mind and help you to achieve that which you affirm. Through affirmations, you envision your goals as though you have already obtained them—an important change of consciousness for success.

Affirmations train the mind in positive thinking. They help you let go of unproductive negative mindsets that hinder you, such as "I never seem to know the right thing to do."

Affirmations are declarations that activate the Law of Mind. According to the philosophy of Science of Mind, founded by Ernest Holmes, we are surrounded by an Infinite Intelligence, or Mind (God), which functions upon our beliefs. If we let go of destructive beliefs and replace them with constructive ones, we enter into a cooperation with this Mind that enables us to be healthier, happier, more successful, and more spiritually fulfilled. To this end, daily affirmations—as well as meditation and prayer—facilitate that objective.

Holmes taught that there is but one Mind and everything is an aspect of It; each of us uses a portion of It. He taught, "My thought is in control of my experience and I can direct my thinking," and "the ability to control my experiences and have them result in happiness, prosperity, and success lies in my own mind and my use of it."

"Mind responds to mind," said Holmes. "It is done to you as you believe." In other words, do not *ask* for things, but *declare* them. This is the Law of Mind, which manifests the beliefs we speak into It."

Affirmations can be applied to any situation or need in life. *I have the perfect and right job for me* is an example of an affirmation that launches a search for a new job. *I enjoy perfect health* is an affirmation that helps us to maintain health as well as to heal.

Here are some affirmations for psychic power:

- *I am psychic*

- *My psychic power speaks clearly to me*
- *My psychic power is always right*
- *I always know what to do*
- *I am always guided to make the right decisions*
- *I receive God's guidance through my psychic power*

Some people feel that affirmations are more powerful when they insert their names into them: "I, Samantha Jones, am psychic," or "I, Samantha, am psychic." I have used affirmations with and without my name and find both styles effective. Use whichever style attracts you.

People sometimes tell me that affirmations don't work for them. They say they use them religiously, but nothing changes.

For affirmations to work, they must penetrate deeply into your consciousness. Many people say affirmations, but they allow them to only float on the surface of their minds, like boats floating on water. Affirmations are like deep probes. They must be sent below the surface into the core of our being. This is the center where conviction is born.

Affirmations work when they anchor deep within your consciousness, where they facilitate change. Affirmations alone do not make change. You must act on your affirmations. It does little good to recite affirmations throughout the day if your words, thoughts, and actions are the opposite. I've known more than a few people who talk affirmations for prosperity, but take no action to improve their finances, and spend a lot of time complaining to others about their poverty.

We must *live* affirmations as well. If your affirmation is to be more financially prosperous, then you must live the affirmation. Do not complain to your friends about your lack and your debt. Making jokes about your debt or making self-effacing, self-critical remarks is counterproductive. Do not descend into envy because your neighbor bought a new car and you can't afford one.

You live the affirmation by doing whatever you can to bring it into manifestation. For financial prosperity, for example, you begin by giving thanks for all the things that you do have, for whatever resources you have. You give thanks for what you can afford. You save. You invest. You look for opportunities to prosper. You set goals and work toward them. You give thanks for your progress. You see the goals as fully realized, *now*.

Norman Vincent Peale, the godfather of the power of positive thinking, said that in order for positive thinking to work, we must believe in our goal in every cell of our being, and picture it as already manifested. Holmes stressed this as well: we must believe with our total being.

When you say, "I am psychic, you must believe it. You must act on it by paying attention and following your guidance.

There are five simple points to remember for success with affirmations:

- Create a clear affirmation.
- Believe in every cell of your being that it is right for you.
- See yourself as having achieved or attained your goal now.
- Ask for guidance and help through your psychic power.
- Do everything you can to create your new reality.

Create – Believe – See – Ask – Do.

Make a commitment to work with affirmations on a daily basis. Create several. Every day, write them out fifteen times each. The repetition will focus your intent and set your psychic consciousness to work on them fulltime. Record your results. You will experience some changes immediately. Other changes may take longer. Be patient and persistent.

For more material on the practical applications of affirmations, see chapter 14.

Give thanks

Whenever you use affirmations and psychic power comes through for you, it is important to give thanks. Thank your Higher Self, the Universe, God. Acknowledging blessings helps to keep a balanced perspective on your connection to the divine, and brings even greater blessings.

Keep an open heart

One facet of psychic power is that it is the wisdom of the heart. It flourishes when you keep an open heart toward yourself, others and life. If you constantly think ill of others, if you are often suspicious of others, if you are always worrying that something dreadful is going to happen, you close your heart. The heart wisdom see potential, not limit. It sees love, not anger or fear.

You can give yourself a quick heart psychic power test anytime. Place your hand over your heart and ask, "From the depths of my heart, is this the right thing for me to do?" Do you feel heavy in the heart, or light? Your heart will give you the answer.

Learn your own Psychic Speak

Everyone experiences psychic power in unique ways. Review Chapter 3 on "Psychic Speak" and do a self-assessment. Even if you are a beginner in psychic development, you will recognize some of the ways that your psychic faculty communicates with you.

Experiment with all of the exercises in Part II. The Keys are designed to awaken and train the psychic faculty in a wide variety of ways. They will reinforce the obvious ways your psychic faculty communicates, and develop the more subtle ways. The more you expand your awareness, the more information you will have to make the best decisions. You will recognize problems much earlier.

Do not be in a hurry to cover all the exercises quickly. Spend time learning them well so that you absorb them.

Pay attention also to your behavior. Take note of what happens to you when you are certain that something is right or wrong. Do you welcome psychic hits, or do you unconsciously shut them down by discounting them?

Keep practicing

The more you practice the exercises, the stronger your psychic power will become. You will begin to use your psychic faculty more pro-actively than reactively.

Let go of attachments to feelings

One of the biggest distractions to psychic functioning is emotion. Attachments to emotions, especially negative ones such as anger, fear, and guilt, prevent you from having access to psychic information, which has no inherent emotion or bias. When strong feelings arise, try to detach yourself from them. Allow them to happen, then let go of them. Be receptive to new feelings that arise—they may surprise you.

Many emotional attachments belong to events or circumstances long past. By living more in the moment, you will be less likely to carry a lot of emotional attachment around with you.

Do your homework

Problems do not solve themselves. Genius does not strike the unprepared. The psychic breakthrough is the extra measure that rewards those who work toward their goals. Great ideas, creativity, and solutions are achieved by examining situations from all possible angles, by applying one's rational knowledge and skill, and by being open to see situations in new and different ways.

Psychic power expands upon a person's abilities, talents, and efforts. A symphony is not likely to fall into the head of someone who hasn't studied music. If you wish to apply your psychic power to making investments, for example, then study the markets. Simple energy healing can be done without knowing much about the body, but if you wish to be a highly skilled medical intuitive, you must learn anatomy and physiology.

Whatever you seek to do in life, psychic power can help you do it better.

James King Hill Jr. made headlines in 2000 when he discovered a huge find of high-quality emeralds in Hiddenite, North Carolina. His success can be attributed to hard work and research, psychic hits, and persistence. He just didn't go out into the hills one day on an inspiration. As he explained to the media, treasure hunting was his first love from childhood. After trying various jobs, he knew he wanted to devote all of his time to hunting for gems. His research told him that his best bet for a good find was Hiddenite, a tiny town about fifty miles from Charlotte, North Carolina, in the Brushy Mountains. Small amounts of gems had been found there, but nobody considered it to be the site of exceptional treasure. Hill had some small strikes, but not the big one that he was convinced was there.

For thirty years, Hill held to his vision. He *knew* the treasure he sought was there. People said he was crazy. He ran out of money and went into debt. Just when things looked their darkest and it seemed like he might be forced to give up, a friend who also was inspired by vision put up the money to give him one more chance. This time, Hill hit pay dirt. The emeralds found were judged among the best in North America.

A research curator of geology made this observation about Hill: "He was very systematic and careful in learning what he needed to know. He found the emeralds he always thought were there."

Fortunately, most of us don't have to persist thirty years to see a psychic vision fulfilled. But Hill's story serves as a good example of following psychic information against the grain of opinion and experience. Hill did his homework, then followed his vision.

Trust your guidance

Your psychic faculty is on target. People sometimes say to me, "Well, my psychic power is usually right, but in this case it wasn't." Wrong. The psychic faculty was right, but was over-ridden by imposed "shoulds," second-guessing, desires, and even fear. Sometimes zeal and enthusiasm are mistaken for psychic hits. We act impulsively instead of intuitively. Or we are so desirous of a particular goal that we convince ourselves a particular course of action is right.

Psychic power must be sought impartially. You cannot get clear guidance if you are wedded to a particular pursuit or idea.

Don't negate, rationalize, or judge your guidance. Examine it. If it conflicts with your projected desires, consider why.

When it comes to making a decision, your fence-sitting, doubts, uncertainty, ambivalence and reservations may be the psychic faculty's way of saying no. It's best not to proceed with a course of action unless you are clear that it is the right course.

If you feel stuck, ask a question and flip a coin. You will either feel elated or disappointed in the result. Upon closer examination, you'll see that your psychic faculty was speaking to you all along.

Psychic power can seem to go beyond logic. Go with it. Albert Einstein attributed some of his greatest ideas to a "free invention of the imagination" rather than to the brainpower of inductive logic. One morning as he arose from bed, Einstein saw in his mind's eye the image of a person riding on a beam of light. From that, he made his breakthrough insight into the relativity of time.

Don't worry about being right

Naturally, you want to make decisions that are right. Sometimes there is a lot at risk. This puts a great deal of pressure on you to be right.

It may seem strange, but in order to be psychic, you cannot be concerned with being right. Your very anxiety will interfere with the psychic process. Fears, hopes, and expectations all have no place in psychic functioning.

You must trust your guidance, and trust that whatever it is, it will be right.

Sometimes the right answer is not what is expected. If you cloud your mind and heart with expectations, you may not hear the truth.

Act on your guidance

Your psychic power is not a complete process until you act on it. Taking action strengthens the psychic faculty. It keeps a positive flow of energy circulating from divine supply through you to manifestation. If you ask the muse for help, you must honor the process in full.

Sometimes acting on guidance isn't easy, especially when you are not certain about where the guidance is taking you. You must trust your faculty.

Lynn felt in a dead end in her job. She had worked in the same field for more than twenty years. She felt she needed a change, but to what? She wasn't certain what else she wanted to do, or even was qualified to do. The idea of retraining for new job skills was daunting. And, she was reluctant to change and risk losing job security and health benefits.

One morning Lynn awakened with these words ringing in her head: *Go back to school.* "It was clear as a bell and very commanding," she told me. "But I thought, why would I want to do that?"

In fact, the idea of going back to school was more intimidating than staying in her stale job. She was in her early fifties and could not envision herself on a campus with much younger students. Wasn't she too old to start over again? And even if she did go back to school, what would she study? How would she pay for it? She certainly couldn't afford to quit her job and go to school fulltime.

Rational objections crowded her mind. Nonetheless, Lynn couldn't shake the idea. It seemed to pop up synchronistically as a reminder. For example, she would be in a conversation, and learn about someone else deciding to go back to school. Or, her attention would be caught by a prominent ad for a college. She would randomly open a women's magazine to a story about loans for second college educations.

Finally, Lynn began to think that perhaps school might be a good idea, but she still didn't know what she would study for another degree. One day she was watching television and a commercial flashed a big advertising slogan on the screen: "Just for fun." The ad did not have anything to do with higher education, but for Lynn, it was a targeted hit.

Just for fun. Suddenly Lynn felt as though a brilliant burst of light went off inside her. Instead of making a commitment to a big plan of study, why not just take a course for the pure fun of it? The idea felt right.

When Lynn had been much younger and in leaner financial times, she had sewn many of her own clothes. She liked sewing, and others had always complimented her on creations. She usually improvised on patterns. She had an eye for putting colors and textures together in novel ways. With work, marriage and home responsibilities, Lynn had given up sewing. In fact, she no longer even had a sewing machine.

"Wouldn't it be fun to take a class in interior decorating?" she thought.

Lynn found an adult education class in interior home design. She would need a sewing machine, but she didn't want to invest in a new one in case the class didn't work out. She found a good used sewing machine at a yard sale.

Lynn thoroughly enjoyed the class. She rekindled her interest in sewing. The talent that she had displayed years ago and which she had dismissed as ordinary shined forth in a new light, impressing students and instructor alike. She became totally absorbed in her art. When a student complimented her by saying, "You're a pro!" Lynn had another insight.

She polished her skill, took some more courses and began doing small jobs for others for nominal fees. She worked at home in the evenings and on weekends. She didn't advertise because she wanted only a small amount of work. Word of mouth, however, brought increasing business.

Her new-found second career gave her a recharge of energy and enthusiasm. Lynn decided not to give up her fulltime job because of its steady income and benefits, and to thus limit her second career as a stylist to projects that she could manage in her available time. She found so much creative fulfillment in her decorating and sewing that her primary job no longer seemed so dull and oppressive.

She realized that her psychic ability had given her just the guidance she needed. It had come in a series of promptings. At first, she had seen her dilemma as all-or-nothing: a complete job/career change. She piled up the negatives. But the signals continued to move her in the right, though unexpected, direction.

Enjoy yourself

Remember that mental concentration must be balanced by relaxation for the psychic faculty to order information for a breakthrough insight. Nourish your ability by taking time to play.

For Nikola Tesla, relaxation often yielded a breakthrough. The inventor of alternating current motors and generators, the radio (wrongly credited to Marconi) and robotics, Tesla was steeped in knowledge about electrical technology. He was highly imaginative, and developed many of his inventions in his imagination.

Tesla received his psychic hit for alternating current while he was out enjoying himself. He had designed a machine that had been ridiculed by one of his professors. He had not yet solved his problem of redesign when he went out one day with a friend. They walked through a park and recited poetry. Tesla was in a good mood and not thinking about his design problem when suddenly the solution hit him. He wrote:

> The idea came like a flash of lightning, and in an instant truth was revealed. I drew with a stick on the sand the diagrams shown six years later in my address before the American Institute of Electrical Engineers. ...The images I saw were wonderfully sharp and clear and had the solidity of metal and stone, so much so that I told [my companion]: "See my motor here, watch me reverse it." I cannot begin to describe my emotions. Pygmalion seeing his statue come to life could not have been more deeply moved. ... For a while I gave myself up entirely to the intense enjoyment of picturing machines and devising new forms. It was a mental state of happiness about as complete as I have ever known in life. Ideas came in an uninterrupted stream and the only difficulty I had was to hold them fast. ... I delighted in imagining the motors constantly running, for in this way they presented to

the mind's eye a more fascinating sight. In less than two months I evolved virtually all the types of motors and modifications of the system which are now identified with my name.

Tesla did his homework by applying his knowledge and rational thought. His psychic hit vaulted him to a new level of insight. Note how his emotions validated his inspiration.

Follow small promptings
One of the most amazing gifts the psychic faculty brings is a strengthening of the bond among human hearts. We have more empathy for others, which enables us to be more charitable, understanding, helpful and forgiving. We are guided to do things for others, especially acts of service and kindness that may seem small to us but have a significant impact on the recipients. Thus, we become better and better channels for the blessings of the Creator to flow through us and out into the world.

You may not always know the outcome of what you are guided to do. You must trust that everything has a perfect place in the harmonious scheme of the universe. The flow of energy—time, love, money, aid, whatever it is you are giving—goes where it is needed. You are part of a delicate and finely tuned cosmic balance. Trusting your psychic sense also means that you trust that you, too, will receive what you need at the right time.

5

Cosmic Connections

Psychic power does much more than help us keep our lives going in the right direction. It connects us to the All That Is. Experiences of psychic insights can be deeply moving, even mystical.

Fields of consciousness

Think of psychic power as your inner desktop organizer. It is your inborn faculty that takes information perceived consciously and unconsciously, sifts through it for salient facts, and organizes it into a form that can be communicated to you in a meaningful way. This is a process that goes on within you all the time.

Not only does your psychic sense organize information about your daily life, it also organizes information related to the whole web of creation. Your own field of consciousness is part of bigger fields that links you to other people, even those whom you do not know and who are at a distance, and to all things, even the world of nature.

This interconnection can be seen in the concept of field consciousness. The old physics taught that objects separated by distance are isolated from one another. Quantum physics has shown us that distance is not a factor in cause and effect. Quantum fields are nonlocal; that is, they are not bounded by time and space. Neither is consciousness.

The idea that consciousness is nonlocal and exists in fields can be found in some of our oldest mystical teachings. The *Upanishads* of Hinduism put forth the idea that there is a single, cohesive underlying reality to everything: Brahman, or the Absolute Self. This single reality unfolds in fields that remain part of the whole and are connected to each other. New physics describes this whole as the implicate order.

Energy, or consciousness, is organized into fields. Morphogenetic fields are fields of energy that organize the forms and behavior of all biological, chemical and physical systems. Once a mathematical abstraction in developmental biology, the idea of morphogenetic fields has been put forward in the last few decades as another model demonstrating that consciousness is not confined by time or space. The fields are rather like the wheel of birth, death and rebirth, in which all things are recycled and reborn anew.

According to Rupert Sheldrake, a British plant physiologist who developed the hypothesis of morphogenetic fields, there is no end or limit to types and numbers of fields, which also include behavioral fields, which are responsible for coordinating instinctive or learned behavior; mental fields, which organize mental activity; social fields, which organize social behavior; and so on. Thoughts and emotions are affected by fields.

The psychic sense, then, functions through various morphogenetic fields, such as mental, emotional, and physical ones. These extensions of ourselves enable us to have connections with people, animals, and places, especially those that we know and care about.

Scientific research into the nature of consciousness has shown that fields of thought, focus, and intention are constantly organizing. In *The Conscious Universe*, Dean I. Radin discusses experiments with random numbers generators to determine the effects of group consciousness established around certain events. Among them were an Academy Awards ceremony, various prime time television shows, broadcasts of the verdict in the O.J. Simpson murder trial, a small workshop, and other events. The random number generators were programmed to produce two bits of information, rather like the flipping of a coin. The results of the experiments showed that during the events, the random number generators produced an ordering of bits greater than chance. The implication is that group consciousness affects order in the physical world.

"The common link between mind and matter, as observed in these experiments, is *order*," said Radin. "Order expressed in the mind is related to focused attention, and order in matter is related to decreases in randomness." Radin further noted that the object of focused attention did not seem to be important—only that a group mind coalesced.

In mysticism, thoughts have a concrete reality. The power of thought can change physical reality. We attract what we think. We become what we think. The power of focused group thought has even greater power to effect change. This is psychokinesis, mind over matter, on a large scale.

Proponents of Transcendental Meditation have attempted to demonstrate this, holding that a sufficient number of people engaged simultaneously in Transcendental Meditation can establish more order by reducing crime, accidents, adverse weather, and so forth. There have been mass experiments to test this with intriguing results.

We are affected by changing fields of consciousness every day, in magnitudes ranging from small to large. Our psychic power is an ordering function, helping us see and understand the implications of these fields—synchronicities, opportunities, and problems. Psychic power helps us move with the flow to our best advantage.

The result of psychic ordering is called luck.

Luck is both made and allowed

We all know people who have gotten big breaks, hit jackpots, won prizes, and come up with winning ideas. With great envy, we say they're lucky: they were born under a lucky sign, the gods smiled on them, it was fate or destiny. They always seem to be in the right place at the right time.

Luck is not a matter of chance. The universe continually presents opportunities to us for growth, abundance, prosperity, and happiness. The natural order of the universe is wholeness, and we are in a constant unfoldment toward that wholeness. Our psychic sense is our guiding star in that unfoldment. It sifts through fields of consciousness and presents us opportunities especially in the form of warnings, nudges and synchronicities.

Luck is what you allow to happen. That doesn't mean that you sit back, relax, and expect the universe to rain blessings upon you. You make your luck by paying attention. Lucky people pay heed to their psychic hits and follow them. They act on them. Lucky people *allow* their luck to unfold. They work, but they work smarter, by letting their psychic power guide them to make the right move at the right time. They know when to persist and when to desist. They see potential where others do not.

When opportunities present themselves, it's not always with banners flying and trumpets blaring. It's often the opposite: a subtle signal, a slight tugging, a whisper. Some people have a natural openness to their psychic side that enables them to hear the subtleties. Others have to work to open up. By developing your psychic power, you will be better able to receive all the guidance being generated all the time by your Higher Self. You will come to *expect* luck as part of your natural order rather than be surprised by it as "chance."

Miracle mindset

When you learn to accept your psychic power and apply it, you are practicing a miracle mindset. Change can be manifested through an alignment of your will with cosmic order and harmony. Psychic development ushers in a major change in consciousness. You see potential, and feel an expansion of your abilities, creativity and power. You have vision and confidence in bringing ideas to fruition. You have a new sense of your purpose and plan in life, that is part of a purpose and plan to the greater whole of creation. You see that God, or the Universal Mind, is the source of all abundance and nourishment. There is no limit to that supply. Each soul has a claim to its own good, which is never diminished by the good obtained by others.

Thus you create within you a miracle mindset. Miracles are not random acts of nature or God, but the *ordered results of change in consciousness.*

"The only qualifications for having a miracle are that one returns one's mind to peace and follows one's inner guidance," states Carolyn Miller, author of *Creating Miracles: Understanding the Experience of Divine Intervention.*

Conscious psychic power

Conscious psychic power is a balance of logic, emotion, instinct and spiritual wisdom. It is part of our evolution, what Robert Ornstein describes in *The Evolution of Consciousness* as a uniting of the insights of the rational, the emotional, the intuitive, and the spiritual:

> "The kingdom of heaven is within" and "Angels are faculties hidden in the mind of man" are ways of describing this unity. Raising consciousness means to become conscious of the different selves within and how they are partial, while also keeping aware of the larger venues of perception.

We need conscious evolution if we are to learn how to survive and thrive in our global village. Conscious evolution will sharpen our psychic skills for solving large-scale problems, and for learning how to get along with our fellow human beings around the planet. Conscious evolution can take us beyond petty differences and expand our awareness so that we see situations more holistically and less selfishly.

Mastery of change and time

Conscious psychic ability will be a critical skill in our ability to adapt to accelerating change. A look at the evolution of life on this planet shows that our entire history is one of shorter and shorter periods between major advancements and change. Our technology is pushing us into shorter and shorter periods, forcing us to adapt to change more quickly. Futurists speculate on our ability to adapt and survive as we grapple with global environmental, racial, cultural, religious, materialist and other self-interest issues. We will only be able to survive and thrive if we evolve on an inner basis. According to futurist Peter Russell in *Waking Up in Time: Finding Inner Peace in Times of Accelerating Change*:

> [I]f we are to survive the critical times we are now passing through, it is essential that we undergo a profound shift in values and awaken to our inner truths and our full spiritual potential. As Buckminster Fuller put it, we are facing our final evolutionary exam. Is the human species fit to survive? Can we develop the consciousness that will allow us to use our prodigious powers with wisdom? If our civilizations continues, it will be because we have

passed the test, and will have already made the step into the exploration of human consciousness.

Russell points out that the only obstacles to inner change are mental: attitudes, mental habits, beliefs about what we should do, and our assumptions about limitations. When we learn how to free ourselves of these fixations, we can change ourselves rapidly.

An important key to inner change is psychic power, which frees us of self-imposed limitations and notions about what we "should" do. Psychic power opens to a limitless horizon.

Businesses have awakened to the need to make fundamental changes in how they conduct their affairs in a global marketplace, where their actions have far greater ramifications than bottom line profits. Even by the 1970s, studies of executives showed that the most successful made use of their psychic power, which they usually referred to as their gut feelings or hunches. Today that power needs to be applied to more than marketing and product development strategies. Today's executives need to be concerned with a company's social and environmental responsibilities, and with employees' desires for greater work satisfaction and meaningful participation in decisions. In other words, the successful business of today and tomorrow must have heart and well as mind.

Psychic power is a leadership and visionary skill that all employees from the top down need to bring to their jobs.

Peaks and plateaus

The experience of psychic hits often brings an expansion, awareness, and bliss that fosters a sense of connection to things on a cosmic level. We have a peak experience. The term "peak experience" was coined by psychologist Abraham H. Maslow, the primary pioneer of humanistic and transpersonal psychologies, to describe nonreligious quasi-mystical and mystical experiences. Peak experiences are a sudden flash of intense happiness and feelings of well-being, and even an awareness of "ultimate truth" and the unity of all things. Peak experiences are accompanied by a heightened sense of control over the body and emotions, and a wider sense of awareness, as though one is standing on a mountaintop. They foster a sense of being lucky or graced; release creative energies; reaffirm the worthiness of life; and change an individual's view of himself.

Maslow described peak experiences as having "a special flavor of wonder, of awe, of reverence, of humility and surrender." The individual, he said, feels "one with the world, pleased with it, really belonging to it, instead of being on the outside looking in... they had really seen the ultimate truth, the essence of things."

These same phenomena flood us in psychic experiences as well. It is important for to have such experiences, for they facilitate the achievement of our full potential. According to Maslow, every human being has innate spiritual yearnings to experience the sacred and fulfill himself to his maximum potential of goodness in terms of healthy living, honesty, creativity, compassion, unselfishness, and so on. Those who do so become "self-actualized": they are mature, healthy, and filled with a zest for living. They have successfully integrated their lower instinctual nature with their higher, godlike nature.

Developing psychic ability helps us to accomplish self-actualization. Psychic experiences are often peak experiences. The experience opens the heart and expands our worldview. Using our psychic power requires an integration and balancing of our lower and higher natures.

Furthermore, using our power expands creativity in all aspects of life. Maslow said that the self-actualized person is happier, healthier, and more creative. Interestingly, he did not equate creativity with great talent, but merely with an ability to do anything, even routine things, creatively.

Maslow said that self-actualized people are more likely to have peak experiences. He coined the term "plateau experience" to describe continuing peak experiences throughout life.

Your life will change for the better

Psychic power is holistic—it draws from, addresses and affects all parts of our being. It is the wisdom of the heart. If you have a sincere desire to become more psychic, be prepared for your entire life to change. You cannot bring the psychic faculty to your job, for example, without it spilling over into your personal life and your spiritual outlook. If you begin by viewing psychic ability strictly as a mental discipline to increase your brain power, you will not contain it there. At some point you will become more sensitive to others, empathically picking up on their thoughts, feelings, and moods. At some point you will become aware of a "higher power" beyond you that has a hand in your life. Using psychic power requires an open heart, and you cannot open your heart without becoming more concerned for and involved with your fellow human beings. You cannot open your heart without pondering and experiencing a profound connection to the Creator.

That's as it should be. Psychic power is part of our path of evolution and soul growth. It combines the best of our instinctual, emotional, and rational brains with our spiritual awareness.

Psychotherapist Belleruth Naparstek found that by having an open heart, her intuitive/psychic ability fosters a profound connection to others which in turn benefits the therapy. In *Your Sixth Sense: Activating Your Psychic Potential*, she said:

> I'm so empathically attuned to my clients when I'm in this state, seeing what they see and feeling what they feel, that I'm aware of an overall, generalized feeling of what I can only described as *love* for them. I'm so suffused with it, I am easily moved by what they say or do with. (This doesn't mean I'm not thinking clearly; on the contrary, my thinking is clearer than usual. That the same time, I am deeply touched by them in this generalized away.) And, where elsewhere in my life I might be critical of their behavior or find fault with their attitudes, in this state compassion crowds out judgment. This doesn't take effort—if it did, I'm sure I'd feel virtuous about it—it just happens.
>
> And most of all, I feel very alive—very present and deeply grateful to be doing this work that I do. A quiet elation fills me as I sit at what has somehow become a glorious kind of meditation.

All of us can experience this love and aliveness. Psychic power increases empathy and compassion and reduces the tendency to criticize and judge. Thus, our relationships to others improve and take on new dimensions and nuances. What's more, when we feel genuine love for others, we experience the miracle of more love flowing back to us.

Says Naparstek:

And from the open heart, we get the true picture of exactly who and what we are. This view is stunning. We've become an enormous energy field that has instantaneous reach everywhere.

Psychic power raises us to a higher level of being. The writings of our great thinkers throughout history, whether they were scientists, politicians, businessmen or mystics, all acknowledge that behind their inspirations is the presence of the Divine.

6

The Holistic Psychic Lifestyle

The exercises in this book will help you develop and polish your psychic skills. There is more to developing psychic power than mental exercises. Using your ability is part of a holistic approach to living. Like plants that flourish when they receive enough light, water and nutrients, the psychic sense flourishes when we nourish all parts of our life—when we are as healthy and vital as possible physically, mentally, emotionally and spiritually.

I recommend that you integrate the following nine-point plan into your daily and regular activities:

1. Get regular physical exercise

Getting regular physical exercise enhances health on all levels. Exercise is especially important for psychic functioning. When you exert yourself, especially in a rhythmic activity, you breathe more deeply. This circulates the universal life force throughout your auric field, and benefits the chakras. As noted in the exercises in Part II, breathing techniques are fundamental to stimulating the psychic faculty.

A profound change in consciousness happens during exercise, perhaps due to the chemicals released in the brain. Athletes are well aware of this shift, and many have reported unusual psychic and mystical phenomena while immersed in their performance. They enter a state of consciousness called "the zone," in which time and space are unbounded. When in the zone, they excel in what they are doing. The zone also is where psychic abilities exist—there are no limits.

These experiences have been well documented by Michael Murphy, co-founder of The Esalen Institute in Big Sur, California, and Rhea A. White, who was a parapsychologist, reference librarian and founder of the Exceptional Human Experience Network. White coined the term "exceptional human experience" to describe 150 types of anomalous, nonordinary experiences of a psychic, mystical and transcendent nature.

In 1972, Murphy published his book *Golf in the Kingdom*, which describes such experiences reported by people while they played golf. In response to the interest in that book, Murphy and White teamed to write *The Psychic Side of Sports*, published in 1978 and revised and reissued as *In the Zone: Transcendent Experience in Sports*, in 1995. They documented about sixty phenomena that occur in more than twenty types of experiences in the zone. Among them are:

- Feelings of power and superiority
- Acute well-being and calm
- Ecstasy; unity
- Altered perceptions of time and space
- Psi
- Out-of-body experiences
- Perceptions of "the other" (such as spirit beings)
- The ability to exert mind over matter, or psychokinesis.

In all, Murphy and White found striking similarities in the extraordinary powers unleashed by sports activity and the extraordinary powers, or *siddhis*, developed through the practice of yoga.

Sports or yoga are not required to unleash these results, however. Recall that Einstein was inspired when he sailed or canoed, and Mozart was inspired when he walked in the woods after dinner.

On another note, you shouldn't undertake physical exercise with the idea that you *will* or *must* have an exceptional or psychic experience. Even running a marathon is no guarantee that an exceptional experience will happen. Holding such an intent defeats the purpose of exercising, which, besides improved health, allows the mind to shift gears and enter an open space.

Pick an activity you like, and exercise for the sheer joy of it. Allow the rest—the psychic and the inspiration—to occur in the right time and place. Sometimes the intuitive flash comes after the exercise.

In concert with your exercise program, pay attention to your nutrition so that you are at peak energy. That also means getting adequate rest. It is hard for the psychic faculty to hammer its way through a mental haze created by fatigue.

2. Meditate daily

Meditation is the stilling of the mind. Primarily a spiritual discipline for spiritual advancement, meditation also has health benefits. Studies show that regular practice of meditation lowers the body's metabolism, slows brainwaves, and induces relaxation. Individuals who meditate regularly show greater resistance to stress and illness, and feel better psychologically.

All of the results produced by meditation are beneficial to psychic power. It is in that stillness that the psychic insights manifest. And, you will have an easier time accessing that ability when you are feeling your best.

There are many techniques for meditation, and students of various spiritual paths can spend years in their practice, perfecting posture, breathing, use of mantra, and transcendence of thought. For years I studied Zen meditation. Though I am much more casual in my approach to meditation today, I still incorporate what I learned from Zen into my personal practice.

If you follow a particular school, continue to use it. If you have not been a meditator, do not be daunted by the thought that you have to learn a complicated system. You can meditate simply by sitting quietly in a chair and quieting the mind. If you do this for even a few minutes every day, you will soon begin to notice changes in your state of well-being, your awareness, and perception of what goes on around you, as well as your psychic faculty. You will become more tuned to subtleties.

As we have seen, detachment is necessary for psychic functioning. You must be detached from outcomes in order to receive the true guidance. Meditation helps to detach from worldly concerns and hear the voice within.

Meditation exercises are given in Key #2 in Part II.

3. Maintain mindfulness

Centuries ago, the great artist Raphael told the great artist and inventor Leonardo da Vinci, "I have noticed that when one paints, one should think of nothing: everything then comes better."

Raphael was expressing the value of mindfulness. When he painted, Raphael did not allow himself to become distracted with thoughts about anything other than what he was doing. In thinking of nothing, he was focusing his full attention upon his art, and all of his energy thus flowed directly onto the canvas.

Most of us live nearly our entire lives somewhere else besides the present. We rehash the past and anticipate the future. All we ever have, however, is *now*. By not living in the now, by not giving ourselves fully to the moment, we let life pass us by.

Mindfulness means devoting yourself to one thing at a time. It means being fully present in what you are doing. Today we rush around, pressed for time, trying to do several things at once. We do paperwork over lunch, shave and apply cosmetics while we drive, listen to an audio book on a headset while we grocery shop, walk across a busy street with our faces glued to a cellphone. Everything gets a fragment of our attention. Does acting like an octopus really make life better? No. We complain more than ever about how pressed we are. We look for ways to become busier and do more faster. No wonder we can't hear the psychic voice within.

Psychic power is a product of the now. It lives in the still point within. Make a commitment to live more in the moment. As you go about your daily affairs, give them your total attention. You will be surprised how much time you spend doing things you do not want to do but feel obliged to do, or how much time you spend in unproductive activity.

When you realize how precious the moment is, you will exercise more care over how you spend your time. You will feel better for it, and become more productive. Being centered and in the moment creates conditions in which intuition can flourish.

Mindfulness also helps you to let go of your attachments to emotions, especially negative ones such as anger, fear, and guilt. Negative emotions inhibit your access to your psychic side. When you live in a state of mindfulness, you can observe the emotions and release them, much the same as you observe thoughts and release them in meditation. Many emotional attachments belong to events or circumstances long past that we keep replaying in our minds. By living more in the moment, you will be less likely to carry emotional attachments around with you.

In Zen, mindfulness is "seeing with the whole mind." We see everything as it really is without effort. We think without effort. Wisdom comes out of mindfulness.

4. Enjoy a beginner's mind

What does it mean to have a beginner's mind? In Zen, it is one of the fundamentals to starting the spiritual work.

Our fast-paced lives bring a been-there-done-that jaded weariness. We are full of expectations, disappointments, cautions, and ambitions which pile up higher and higher as we go through life. We see fewer and fewer possibilities and opportunities. Once upon a time, life seemed much easier. If only we could turn back the clock and start over again.

All it takes to revitalize your outlook on the world is beginner's mind.

Beginner's mind constantly sees the world as new. Instead of limit there is limitlessness. Instead of doubt there is openness. No matter how often something is done—a task, a chore, the recitation of a prayer—the beginner's mind experiences it as if for the first time every time, knowing that no two experiences are ever the same.

Wayne W. Dyer describes this as a sense of total and complete awe. When we practice being in awe daily—holding a reverence for all life and giving thanks for what we take for granted—we soon enter a state of enlightenment. "Enlightenment is simply the silent acceptance and appreciation for what is," Dyer says. "Be enlightened and miracles will be your way of life."

Beginner's mind is akin to the archetype of The Fool in the Tarot. The Fool is not a person who is ignorant and reckless, but one who is willing to be open to all possibilities. The Fool has no prejudices, no habits. The Fool looks out on a world of unbounded opportunity and adventure. He has a natural mind and is constantly filled with wonder.

This doesn't mean that the lessons and wisdom of experience should be dismissed. But if you keep your outlook fresh and open, you are more vibrant, expressive, creative, and inventive. You see your place and importance in the whole cosmic scheme of things.

Mindfulness and beginner's mind go hand in hand.

5. Appreciate nature

Make it a point to spend some time in nature as often as possible. Sit outdoors during lunch, go for a walk in a park, or spend a weekend in the mountains or at the seashore. Nature is conducive to peak and mystical experiences. The great philosopher William James was 57 years old when he went hiking in the Adirondack Mountains. There, he was swept up in spiritual experiences which he described as a meeting in his breast between all the gods of the nature mythologies and the moral gods of the inner life. He intuited truths that had eluded him intellectually. The experiences inspired much of the content of his classic work, *The Varieties of Religious Experience: A Study in Human Nature*, and also stimulated his interest in the paranormal.

When you are out in nature, practice mindfulness and beginner's mind. Experience everything around you as though for the first time. Take in your environment through your senses, one by one. Gaze at a flower and appreciate its beauty in detail. Think no particular thoughts but enjoy what nature has to offer.

The great inventor Michael Faraday credited some of his greatest inspirational leaps to time spent in nature doing "idle wool-gathering" which had no object other than pleasure:

> A sensitive mind will always acknowledge the pleasures it receives from a luxuriant prospect of nature; the beautiful mingling and gradations of color, the delicate perspective, the ravishing effect of light and shade, and the fascinating variety and grace of the outline, must be seen to be felt; for expressions can never convey the ecstatic joy they give

to the imagination, or the benevolent feeling they create in the mind. There is no boundary, there is no restraint 'til reason draws the rein.

In addition, practice the Expanded Listening exercise described in Key #6 in Part II. The exercise will help you listen to the subtle undercurrents of nature.

7. Read spiritual literature

The great sacred texts of the world's religions and philosophies provide rich nutrients for the psychic faculty. They embody our highest ideals, ethics, values, and understandings of Truth.

In addition, the writings of the world's great mystics contain a powerful spiritual force that opens up the consciousness. Mystics write from an intense level of inspiration and Truth—they are literally pens in the hand of God. So inspired are they that some mystics seem difficult to comprehend, at least with left-brain thinking. To get the most out of the mystics, one should approach them from an open, receptive frame of mind. The wisdom of the mystics is absorbed rather than learned. In an alchemical fashion, it sinks deep into consciousness, where it works and bubbles away to later burst forth in an illumined thought, inspiration, or revelation.

Spiritual literature trains consciousness to be receptive to the Divine Mind. As the medieval German mystic Jakob Boehme said:

> When both thy intellect and will are quiet and passive to the expressions of the eternal Word and Spirit, and when thy soul is winged up above that which is temporal, the outward senses and the imagination being locked up by holy abstraction, *then* the eternal Hearing, Seeing, and Speaking will be revealed in thee.

Pick a sacred text or collection of mystical writings and keep it as a bedside companion. Read a little every night before you sleep. You will finish your day and enter your night in a much more relaxed state. And, you will fertilize the field of your dreams, another rich source of psychic guidance.

7. Pay attention to your dreams

As we saw earlier, the psychic faculty often speaks through dreams. I have done dreamwork for the better part of my life, and I believe that dreams are one of our best and richest sources of spiritual, creative, and practical guidance. Psychic power uses dreams to get across powerful messages and great ideas.

We all dream nightly, and we have multiple dreams throughout our sleep cycle. Most of us remember only the dream we are having prior to waking up. Some people naturally have sharper dream recall than others. Some have a difficult time remembering dreams, and may think they do not dream at all. However, scientific research has demonstrated that we do dream, whether we remember them or not, or we would become ill. Studies in which people are deprived of their dream sleep show that health suffers when we don't dream.

Your dreams are a voice of your Higher Self. Acknowledging dreams and asking them to reveal more to you will often stimulate a response of increased dream awareness and recall.

Many people don't pay much attention to their dreams because on the surface they seem strange and inscrutable. Yet dreams reveal themselves quite easily when we catch on to how they communicate. Dreams speak in symbols and images. Sometimes their meaning is quite obvious to us. Other times we can use a variety of techniques such as free association and meanings of universal symbols to help us interpret them.

Dreams are mirrors of Truth. They make use of images from daily life—things we have done recently—and also draw upon archetypal images as well. Everyone should have an understanding of his or her dream life in order to get the full benefit of psychic insights. Try the dream incubation in Key #12 in Part II to learn how to ask your dreams for specific guidance. For more about dreamwork, see my book *Dreamwork for Visionary Living*.

8. Use music medicine

A holistic diet for the psychic faculty includes a sound diet as well. The powerful effects of music upon mind, body, and spirit have been known and used since ancient times. Modern research is demonstrating what our distant ancestors already knew: music heals, inspires, soothes, and opens the gateways to breakthrough experiences.

The ancient Chinese believed music to be the basis of everything: all things, including man, were molded according to the music that was performed within them. Confucius stated that if the music of a kingdom changed, then its society would alter itself accordingly. Plato, too, believed that music had the power to affect the fortunes of a nation. The Greeks used music extensively in healing.

Modern studies have documented how music affects biochemical and hormonal processes and neuromuscular activity, and suppresses pain-conducting structures in the brain stem. Music therapy is used to treat a wide range of physical and psychological conditions, and to treat pain. Music also can help to induce altered states of consciousness that produce peak and mystical experiences and psychic flashes of insight and creativity. It can help us to absorb more information when we read.

Researchers have discovered that the music of Mozart is particularly beneficial to well-being and creativity. As musicologist Don Campbell reports in *The Mozart Effect*, "the rhythms, melodies and high frequencies of Mozart's music stimulate and charge the creative and motivational regions of the brain."

Musicology is a fascinating topic and is well worth study to learn more about how sound and vibration affect us physically, mentally, and emotionally. Too often, we are mindless about the sounds with which we surround ourselves. We turn on music more as background noise, and we often think the louder it is the better. While music has been shown to help us, studies also show that the wrong kind of sound and music—especially loud, discordant sounds and heavy, low vibrations of sounds—can adversely affect our health.

Music is part of our holistic diet, a potential source of nourishment for the body, mind, spirit–and psychic ability.

Here are nine points for using music to enhance your psychic power:

- *Work with music you like.* Play familiar music that pleases you and reflects the mood you want to be in. Avoid music that has unhappy or negative associations. Learn how different pieces energize you or relax you. Music that lowers your pulse rate has a beat of sixty beats per minute or less, is played on strings and woodwinds, and has no lyrics. Music that is more stimulating has a faster tempo and has prominent brass and drums. Lyrics stimulate by engaging emotions and thought processes.

- *Pay attention to your breathing and body.* When music relaxes you, your breathing becomes deeper and more regular. If your breathing becomes shallow or irregular, the music is agitating your body. If you feel pain, discomfort, music is having negative affect.

- *Take music baths.* Music is most effective when it is experienced in its fullness. Rather than play music only as background for activity, set aside time regularly to do nothing but listen to music with total awareness. Think of the music as washing over you. Breathe into the music, let your body be carried by it. Become one of the instruments. When you're done, you'll feel light, energized and relaxed.

- *Keep a musical notebook.* By recording how different types of music and individual compositions affect you physically, emotionally and spiritually, you will gain a better understanding of the impact of music on your health. Keep a discography of composers and selections and your response to them.

- *Take a "sound inventory" of your home.* The body reacts to all sounds around it. Music will be much more effective if you minimize or eliminate distracting noises such as appliances and outside sounds. Take your music baths in the quietest room in the house. Use music to mask noises you cannot reduce or eliminate.

- *Use imagery and positive thinking.* Music can enhance your energy and creativity if you give yourself positive suggestions and affirmations while listening to appropriate selections. Visualize yourself accomplishing a goal. If you're faced with a problem, ask for help. The answer may come to you while you listen. If relaxation is your goal, visualize your favorite peaceful setting.

- *Let music enhance your daily activities.* To get off to a fresh and brisk start each morning, play music with a lively rhythm. Unwind at the end of the day with selections that are soft and soothing. Play relaxing music during dinner to aid digestion. Listen to more relaxing music just before you retire to help you sink into a deep and peaceful slumber.

- *Let music enhance your meditation.* You may prefer to meditate in silence, but music can deepen the experience by preparing you for silence by quieting your mind and body and allowing you to be more receptive to the divine. Such pieces are discovered over time and through careful listening. Used regularly for meditation, music can help you attain a receptive state of mind much more quickly.

- *Play a musical instrument.* Many of us learn to play an instrument in childhood, then give it up later in life. Something extra happens when you play a musical instrument that does not occur just by listening. The instrument and music become part of you. And, most instruments require a certain amount of arm movement or deep breathing, which is good exercise. It doesn't matter if you aren't a professional-caliber musician. Play for the sheer pleasure.

Part II
Keys for Developing Your Psychic Power

Introduction to the Keys

This section features twenty-two Keys, or tools, which comprise a comprehensive plan to open, increase, and hone your psychic skill. Within the keys are multiple exercises. Altogether, the twenty-two Keys have ninety-five exercises. All the physical senses are addressed.

Each key has its own unique role in your intuitive unfoldment. Most of them can be done by yourself. A few require partners.

Keys one through twelve cover different approaches to the intuition, and get you comfortable with expanding your unseen senses. Keys thirteen through twenty-two are especially helpful for improving your accuracy.

You will excel at some techniques more than others. Go through all the keys before you settle on the techniques you wish to work with the most. Incorporate the keys into your holistic intuitive living.

Key #1

Psychic Power Breathing

The first and most important thing to learn in developing your psychic power is a good breathing technique. The breath is not just the medium for taking oxygen into the body, but serves as the medium for distributing the universal life force through the body. The universal life force governs health and well-being, and permeates all things. As mentioned earlier, it is known as *prana*, *qi*, *ki*, *mana* and other terms. When our ability to absorb universal life force is good, we are healthy and vital. When our ability to absorb it becomes poor or impaired, our health suffers. Good breathing techniques help to circulate the universal life force throughout the body.

The universal life force also penetrates the aura through the chakras, which, in Eastern spirituality, are whirlpool-like interfaces that assimilate *prana* into all of our energetic layers: the physical, mental, emotional, and spiritual bodies. We have numerous chakras, and there are seven primary ones that are aligned approximately along the spine. Each chakra governs physical, emotional, and spiritual functions, including those that relate to good intuition and psychic ability.

Breathing techniques help to keep the chakras clear and open. Numerous breathing techniques have been developed, especially in the Eastern arts of meditation and medicine. Some of them are complicated. I have tried a variety of them myself, sitting or standing in certain positions, breathing through alternate nostrils, holding my tongue in certain positions, and so on. They are all effective, but I still felt a need to develop something simple and practical that most people could incorporate into their daily routine. The result is the Psychic Power Breathing, below.

Exercise #1: Psychic Power Breathing

This technique is so simple you can do it anywhere. Take three long, slow, and deep breaths. Breathe in through your nostrils. You can either breathe out through your nostrils or your mouth. As you breathe, focus on these:

1. Breathe... *slow down*.

When we're trying to solve a problem or make a decision or get ideas, the mind races. Thoughts run in all directions. The first breath is to rein in that distraction.

2. Breathe... *center*.

Pull in your energy and focus the breath in the body. Be fully present in the moment. The second breath is to gather your inner resources.

3. Breathe... *release and expand*.

As you exhale on the third breath, be aware that the Higher Self is now in charge. Space has been made in your consciousness for intuition to reveal what you need to know.

In three breaths, you will find yourself remarkably composed and in a different state of consciousness. Psychic Power Breathing employs esoteric magic as well. In numbers mysticism, three represents the ascent of consciousness to higher planes. It's a door-opener to the realm of the gods. When we use the number three with a mindfulness in meditative exercises, we are seeking higher wisdom. This is why we find three so often in tales of mysticism and magic: charms are recited three times; we are given three wishes; and so on.

Think of this technique as represented by the upward-pointing triangle which rests on the earth (the physical plane) and points to the heavens (intuitive wisdom). The breath brings our mind, body and spirit into harmony and balance so that the heavens can be reached.

Exercise #2: Alchemical Breathing

This technique came out of my energy healing training, and made me a believer in the role of breathing in the development of psychic power. I found that when I used it, my sixth sense opened more quickly and with greater sensitivity. The more I used it, the faster I progressed. What's more, the simplicity of it encouraged me to use it daily, anywhere or any time, sitting or standing, alone or in the midst of people. I call it Alchemical Breathing because it reminds me of old alchemical images that depict the circulation of vital energies between heaven and earth in the process of wholeness and enlightenment.

Alchemy is a western mystery path of enlightenment. Many people think of alchemists as persons who tried to turn lead into gold. Some alchemists did indeed pursue that goal, but the physical gold was a metaphor for the spiritual gold of enlightenment, attained through processes of purification. The development of the intuition is part of alchemy, as it is any path of enlightenment.

The original purpose for which I learned this breathing technique was bioenergy healing. My teacher, Mietek Wirkus, taught it as a way to quickly raise the level of the universal life force for the purpose of healing through the hands. Energy healing involves sensing and working with the subtle energies of the chakras and aura, which must be done on an intuitive level.

Out of all of breathing techniques I have ever tried, I've found this one to be the best. If you want to put yourself on a psychic fast track, I recommend that you learn and use Alchemical Breathing on a frequent basis.

Here's how it works:

First imagine that you are in oval shaped bubble. As you breathe in and out, you will visualize yourself pushing the breath up and down and around this bubble, anchored around two chakra points.

The starting point is the root chakra at the base and back of the spine. As you draw in your breath, visualize it traveling from the root chakra up the spine to the base of the back of the head, at the point where the head meets the spine. There is a powerful chakra point there. Then hold the breath briefly and visualize it traveling from the base of the head through the head to the forehead between your brows, which is the point of the sixth chakra. As the breath is exhaled, visualize it pouring from the sixth chakra down the front of the body back to the root chakra. Hold the breath briefly again, and visualize pushing from the front of the root chakra to the back of the spine. Breathe in and start the circulation cycle over again.

All of the breathing is done through the nostrils. Inhale deeply into the belly. When you exhale, push the breath out from the belly. As it exits through the nostrils, allow it to rattle at the back of the palate, as though you were going to make a snorting noise.

The inhalation, exhalation, and holding of the breath is done in a ratio of two to one: 4/2, 6/3 or 8/4. For example, breathe in for the count of eight, hold the breath for the count of four, breathe out for the count of eight, hold the breath for the count of four, and so on.

The shorter the ratio cycle, the faster the universal life force is circulated, and the faster the energy is raised. In the beginning, it is good to practice with an 8/4 or 6/3 ratio. When you are comfortable with the technique, try the 4/2 ratio.

Now give it try.

Stand with your spine straight. Relax your body. Become aware of your breathing. Most of us breathe too shallowly. You will probably find that your breath doesn't go down into the belly. Take a few deep breaths and push the air down as far as possible, expanding your belly as you breathe in.

Place your point of concentration at the root chakra. Now breathe deeply and begin the cycle with a count of eight. Pull the breath energy up the spine counting to eight... hold the breath and push the energy from the back of the head through the third eye counting four... expel the breath down to the root chakra counting eight... hold the breath and push from front of the root chakra to the back counting four... and being again.

Do the entire cycle three times.

How do you feel? If you are not accustomed to breathing deeply, you may feel a little tingling sensation or some light-headedness. These sensations will diminish the more you practice. Take your time and go at a comfortable pace.

Do ten complete cycles. You should feel refreshed and energized. Some people feel some discomfort, even a slight headache. This may be due to the circulation of sluggish energy in the sixth chakra at the brow. The more you practice this breathing technique, the more symptoms are likely to diminish.

Now that you understand the process, try adding another element that will benefit the circulation of energy in the third eye. As you exhale, rattle the breath in the back of the palate, as though you were going to exhale through the mouth but push the breath out through the nostrils instead. Continue to visualize the breath energy pouring out of the third eye on the exhale.

Do five more cycles.

Give yourself a little rest. Now try the breathing to a shorter counting cycle: 6/3. Breathe in and out to a count of six and hold the breath to a count of three. Do three complete cycles.

Give yourself another little rest. This time, shorten the counting cycle to 4/2. Do three complete cycles. You will notice that the longer counting cycles make you feel more relaxed, while the short cycle raises a lot of energy. Healers who use this breathing technique often do the short cycle as a way of maximizing the flow of energy to the patient. For the purposes of intuition, I find that the longer cycles work better. I use the 6/3 most often. Over time, you will find that you no longer need to keep a precise count, and you can do the breathing naturally.

Alchemical Breathing can be done either standing or sitting. Do ten cycles to start the day. It's also a good idea to do it throughout the day, such as when you are standing in line or sitting at a desk. It's a great way to refresh your energy and concentration at any time. Of course, do a few breaths before undertaking any psychic development exercise. If you simply use this breathing technique on a daily basis, you'll find your intuition and psychic power to be clearer and more responsive.

Key #2

Meditation Adventures

Breathing techniques and regular meditation are the two most important activities you can do to encourage the expansion of your psychic ability. If you think that meditation requires you to be a loin-clothed, fasting yogi sitting for hours in a lotus position, you've got the wrong impression. There are many styles of meditation. You can make it enjoyable and interesting, even if you spend only fifteen or twenty minutes at it. For the best results and the fastest progress, daily is the ideal frequency. If you're not in the habit of daily meditation, do it as often as you can every week. It's not an all-or-nothing proposition. Once you see the benefits of it, you'll want to meditate daily.

You don't need a special room, clothing, mats, or cushions. Wear your regular clothing and use a comfortable chair or sofa for seating. It is helpful to have a quiet place. If you have a busy family, find a spot in an unused room or go into your bedroom.

I find that meditation in the morning is best. It is worth getting up a little earlier in order to do it. Meditation freshens the mind, calms and centers, and is a great way to start the day. Nighttime prior to sleep is also good. Many people find time to meditate during their workday, such as lunch breaks. They close the door to their office or find a spot outdoors. Some even sit in their cars. I have meditated many times on planes, trains and buses.

The purpose of meditation is to still the mind so that one can achieve a breakthrough of consciousness to a higher spiritual level. From the standpoint of the intuition and psychic power, meditation stills the busy mind and clears the decks for the breakthrough of insight.

Meditation uplifts the mind and soul so that you are functioning on the highest possible level of being. Regardless of how you wish to use your intuition and psychic power, know that your ability comes from the source of divine Truth. The higher you set your sights, the clearer the guidance for your best good.

Meditation is like planting and fertilizing a crop. For a while, it may seem that nothing happens. Then suddenly new growth sprouts above the surface.

Meditation also will take you below the surface into your own depths. The results of that journeying—the crop of intuitive insights—will spring forth at the appropriate time.

Sometimes, however, meditation spontaneously takes on a life of its own. When that happens, go with it and allow it to unfold. You may find yourself hearing, seeing, or being shown or given things. Accept, acknowledge, observe. Analyze and interpret later.

At the end of every exercise, always give thanks for the experience. Intuitive results may not be apparent immediately, but they will unfold. Gratitude is empowering. It acknowledges our gifts from within and from the realm of spirit.

Exercise #1: Sitting Meditation

Sit in a comfortable place, for you will remain more alert if you are seated. Lying down, you may become so relaxed that you fall asleep. Keep your spin as straight as possible. Allow the body to relax by breathing deeply and slowly. Use Psychic Power Breathing.

Close your eyes. Visualize a stream of white and gold light entering your head through the crown chakra. Give it a name: the Universal Life Force, the Love of God, the Boundless Supply, or whatever spontaneously comes to mind. This is your connection to all creation, to all wisdom, to all knowing. Allow the light to permeate the body. Send it through each of your chakras... the third eye... the throat... the heart... the solar plexus... the spleen... the root. Send it to all your body parts... your organs... your skin... your connective tissue... your muscle... your bones... your arteries and vessels... your nerves... your cells. Allow the light to flow out through your feet, into the ground... into the planet. You are now fully connected and grounded: open to the heavens above and planted in the earth below.

Quiet your thoughts as much as possible. The mind is busy, and even when you are relaxed, a continual mental chatter flows through the mind, which wants to wander. As thoughts arise let them go, like balloons drifting away on a wind, or water running through a sieve. The challenge is to not be distracted by thoughts and not get caught up in them. As you release your thoughts, gently sink deeper and deeper into a tranquil state of consciousness. Become a feather drifting downward through the air. When you come to rest, find profound peace.

Be present to the peace and stillness. Be filled with the white and gold light. Nothing more. When thoughts arise, let them go, softly, gently. Some days it takes longer to quiet the mind than others. No matter. You simply keep releasing. Do not try to stop your thoughts from originating—they are "mind waves," as they are called in Zen, and they pass.

If thoughts become particularly intrusive, recenter by focusing on your breathing. Count the breath on the exhale up to fifteen. Start over again if necessary, and repeat as many times as necessary. Above all, stay relaxed. Some days are more productive for meditation than others. Do the best you can.

Stay in your meditative state for twenty minutes. If you are new to meditation, this may seem like a very long time. The more you meditate, however, the longer you will be able to sit and the deeper you will be able to go.

Return from your meditation by taking three deep breaths. Push the air out vigorously through the nose or mouth. Push energy out through your feet and feel the solid connection to earth. Feel firmly centered in your body. Open your eyes.

You may wish to spend some time journaling after meditation. Sometimes the fruits of meditation appears later. Pay attention.

Exercise #2: Open-eyed Meditation

Most people naturally want to close their eyes for meditation. In Zen, however, one keeps them open. This is to remind us that we are part of the world around us, but detached from it. With eyes open, we are less likely to get sleepy and to produce daydream-like mental imagery. And, we are aware of what is going on in our environment, but we are not disturbed by it.

Try meditating with your eyes open. You will find it to be a much different meditational experience than with eyes closed. Perhaps you will even like it better.

Follow the steps in the Sitting Meditation. Instead of closing your eyes, keep them open and cast slightly downward, as though at about a forty-five-degree angle. Do not look at anything in particular. As in the Sitting Meditation, release thoughts and recenter as necessary. If activity enters your field of vision, treat it as you would thought and allow it to pass.

The zendo (meditation hall) I once belonged to in Rye, New York, met in a Quaker church. The church was next door to the fire station. It was not unusual for our meditation to be punctured by blaring sirens and trucks screaming out of the garage. It was a wonderful discipline to maintain the still center with such distraction. Anyone can meditate in a quiet place. A true meditator can meditate anywhere, in the midst of commotion, and attain a state of enlightened consciousness.

Exercise #3: The Pearl of Wisdom Meditation

Jewels symbolize spiritual truths and wisdom, and the reflection of divine light. In myth and folk tale, a search for jewels represents a spiritual quest. To possess jewels is to possess knowledge and enlightenment.

In this exercise, you will work with the pearl, the special symbol of wisdom, as a doorway to the intuition. In esoteric lore, pearls represent the feminine principle, which in turn is associated with right-brain intuitive arts. Pearls once were sacred to the Mother Goddess. "Pearls of wisdom" were given out by Aphrodite Marina (Venus of the Sea) through her priestesses. As late as the Renaissance, it was believed that pearls were formed by an interaction between the sea and the moon, thus giving them strong associations with the lunar-governed forces of intuition, emotion and the unconscious.

The pearl is also used in Zen as a symbol of perfection.

Follow the steps for Sitting Meditation. When you reach the still center, visualize a gleaming pearl hung in the black sea of space. Observe it carefully. Notice its color and glow, its smooth surface. Float around it in space, viewing the entire surface.

Merge with the pearl. Become one with the Pearl of Wisdom.

Using the breath, recenter in your body.

Make notes about your experience. What happened when you became one with the Pearl of Wisdom?

Exercise #4: The Jewel in the Crown Meditation

This exercise is an advanced variation of the Pearl of Wisdom exercise. It is more active than the previous two exercises.

Instead of a pearl, you will work with an emerald in a crown. Jewels in a crown symbolize supreme wisdom. Your crown is of gold, the symbol of enlightenment.

The emerald is a powerful symbol in the Western mystery tradition. It represents all knowledge and Truth—everything that can be known but perhaps not expressed. Truth cannot always be put into words; it is experienced in the heart and intuited on a soul level.

The emerald has association with the Mother Goddess, especially in her vegetation aspect. Thus, it represents the renewal of the Earth, and also immortality. In Biblical lore, the emerald was one of four stones given by God to Solomon.

The Holy Grail, the symbol of the mysteries of Christ and the illumined heart, is often described as an emerald or other jewel, as well as a cup or chalice.

The emerald also is a central image in the mystical path of Western alchemy. According to myth, Hermes Trismegistus ("Thrice greatest Hermes") was the greatest of all philosophers, the greatest of all kings, and the greatest of all priests. He is said to have reigned for 3226 years. He carried an emerald or emerald tablet upon which was recorded all of philosophy, knowledge and the magical secrets of the universe.

Hermes Trismegistus is credited with writing forty-two sacred books (by some accounts many more) conveying the teachings of the gods. Most likely the books were authored between the third century BC and the first century AD—or even later, well into the Middle Ages—by various anonymous persons in succession who signed them "Thoth" to give them weight and the appearance of antiquity.

This corpus, collectively known as the Hermetica, was housed in the great library in Alexandria. Most of them were lost when the library was burned by Christians in 48 BC. Surviving books were protected by initiates. Lore holds that the axiom of the Western mysteries, "That which is above is like that which is below," is inscribed on the Emerald Tablet. The axiom means that the realm of the gods is mirrored on earth, and the external world is a reflection of the inner world. The axiom teaches that what we are on the inside–what we are spiritually–creates our material circumstances.

In dreams, emeralds often represent higher wisdom, especially if they are in the form of crown jewels or emerald eyes.

Gold symbolizes the sun, divine light, divine fire, illumination, the highest state of glory, and the Word of God or Truth. In alchemy, gold represents the attainment of the Philosopher's Stone, or enlightenment. It is the color of the masculine principle of the cosmos. Thus, in this exercise we have the masculine and feminine cosmic principles joined together over the third eye of intuitive and visionary sight.

Begin the Jewel in the Crown Meditation by following the steps for the Sitting Meditation. When you reach the still center, hold a vision of yourself radiant and filled with the white and gold light.

Allow yourself to become crowned with a beautiful band of gold. In the center of the crown is a large and brilliant emerald. Perhaps the crown simply appears on your head. Perhaps it descends from heaven. Perhaps it is given to you by an angel or spiritual being.

In your mind's eye, stand outside yourself and observe your crown and stone. Is the crown simple or ornately carved? Are there symbols upon it? What is the cut of the gem? Feel the weight of the crown resting upon your forehead. Feel the radiance of the emerald. The energy of the crown and its jewel flow down the forehead to the third eye, and then down through the body, its emerald light mixing with the white and the gold.

Affirm to yourself silently, *I am illumined. I see Truth.*

Feel yourself permeated with the presence of Truth. Rest in this field of energy.

When you feel ready, recenter your consciousness with the breath and open your eyes.

Know that the Crown of Wisdom is part of you and that you always wear it.

Spend a few minutes journaling about your experience.

Exercise #5: The Chalice of Higher Wisdom Meditation

In this exercise, you sit in the silence and become a receptacle, or Holy Grail, to be filled with the Divine Mind. When you enter deep silence, you become inspired with fresh resolve, new creative thought, solutions to problems, and understandings of Truth.

The Holy Grail legend has many stories associated with it. In Christianity, the grail represents the mystery of resurrection. The grail itself is a mystery, often described as a jeweled cup or chalice, or as a precious stone. In perhaps the best-known version of the legend, the grail is a cup that Joseph of Arimathea used to catch the blood of Christ as he was pierced with a spear on the cross. After the crucifixion, Joseph took the grail to England and hid it in the area of Glastonbury.

In Arthurian lore, the grail symbolized the spiritual quest. At one Pentecost, the knights of King Arthur were gathered around the Round Table, and a vision appeared floating over them of the grail and the dove of the Holy Spirit. The knights vowed to go in search of this grail. In their quest, they experienced obstacles, successes, and failures, just as we all do as we go through life.

The grail also is a symbol found universally in myth—that of the cup of unending, eternal spiritual replenishment. When you drink from the grail, you take in the nourishment from the Source of All Being.

Follow the procedures for the Sitting Meditation. As you fill yourself with the white and gold light, visualize a luminous chalice within you. The chalice is centered in the heart. When the heart is illumined, we have found Truth; we are connected to divine wisdom. Observe the chalice. What does it look like? Is it jeweled or inscribed? Is it on a tall stem or a short base?

Visualize and feel the white and gold radiance filling your chalice. There is no limit to how much your chalice can hold. Know that within the radiance is everything you need to know. It will reveal itself to you when the time is right.

Affirm to yourself silently, *My heart is illumined. I am filled with Truth.*

As the light pours into your chalice, you are refreshed and revitalized. When you feel ready, recenter with the breath and open your eyes.

Know that the Chalice of Higher Wisdom is always within you. It is filled with an unlimited supply of spiritual wisdom, Truth, and nourishment.

Exercise #6: Walking Meditation

Walking meditation is a refreshing change from sitting meditation. It moves spiritual energy through the body, which is important for nourishing the intuition.

Walking meditation can be done informally, such as a stroll through a garden or park or along the beach. It can be done as a walk through your neighborhood. It can also be done as a more formal ritual. However you choose to walk your meditation, it should be undertaken with *mindfulness*.

Prepare yourself for Walking Meditation by following the steps in Sitting Meditation for breathing and relaxing the body. Fill yourself with the white and gold light, and establish the connection to the heavens and the earth.

If you are walking informally, pace yourself slowly. Be aware of the connection of your feet to the ground. Use each of your senses to experience as much detail as possible around you. Try not to think of the past or the future; simply be present to the moment and the environment around you.

For a more formal Walking Meditation ritual, try the *kinhin* walking meditation of Zen. Once you are relaxed and centered and connected to the heavens and the earth, stand and take the *kinhin* walking posture. Make a loose fist with your left hand and place it over the solar plexus. Place your right hand over it in a gentle cup. This will push your elbows out from the body. Drop the shoulders to relax them. Keep the spine straight. Step forward with your right foot. Steps are taken very slowly, as though in slow motion. Your intent is to experience a deep contact with the earth. Plant each foot and pause for a second or two, then slowly lift the foot and move forward. Keep your eyes cast downward at the forty-five-degree, half-mast angle.

Kinhin can be done indoors in a circumambulation around a room. The movement of the body brings new awareness that might have lain dormant while sitting.

Do a walking meditation at least once a week. One of my favorite variations is to do this indoors, with Gregorian chant music playing in the background. Gregorian chant is a body of more than 3000 works of sung psalms, hymns, and prayers. Composed in Latin, Gregorian chant flourished in monasteries during medieval times. It is a timeless style of music, calling to the monk in every soul. It brings one's total attention to the moment.

I begin with a period of sitting meditation and then do walking meditation. I finish with a short sitting meditation. I find that walking to Gregorian chant is especially consciousness-expanding in nature.

Exercise #7: The Great Seal Meditations

Buddhism teaches many ways to hold and poise the mind in meditation. Mahamudra ("Great Seal") meditation was practiced by the early Dalai Lamas of Tibet. Through it, one comes into an understanding of the true nature of the mind.

Mahamudra meditation is taught in metaphors. There are various mahamudra traditions; Buddha is credited with teaching the first. The following six pointers are common to most of the mahamudra traditions. Try them as a way of stilling the mind:

> *#1: The mind should be kept like the sun in a cloudless sky.* The mind is like clear light, which is knowingness. Clouds represent wandering, distraction, torpor, and so on. When the clouds appear, let the sun disperse them gently so that they disappear.

> *#2: The mind should be like an eagle soaring in the sky.* The eagle is graceful and powerful in the way in soars in flight with very little effort. Let the mind soar in luminous awareness.

> *#3: The mind should be kept as the image of the ocean, deep and tranquil.* Disturbances—thoughts and phenomena—

appear like ripples and waves on the surface. Let the mind become as the ocean when it appears as glass, smooth and calm.

#4: The mind should be like a child in a temple. A child has the ability to see an entire panorama and is open to the big view. Do not let the mind get bogged down by small details.

#5: The mind should be like a bird in flight leaving no footprint. The phenomena of the senses—heat and cold, pain, sound, rushes of energy and other sensations—are like the footprints of the bird. They must be left behind in the flight of the mind. Be not attached to phenomena. Allow them to rise and fall away.

#6: The mind should be like a dandelion fluff in the autumn, picked up by the wind. The mind should be kept light and buoyant. If the mind becomes heavy because of fatigue or the discomfort of the body, move the body slightly to restore the lightness.

You'll undoubtedly learn other meditation techniques besides the ones given here. Add those that work well for you to your repertoire. Keep your practice varied so that it doesn't become stale or predictable to you. Let meditation always be an adventure.

Key #3

Chakra Energizing

Like Key #1, Psychic Power Breathing, this exercise is one of the basic essentials in your intuition training program. It will help you to:

- become familiar with the chakras and their functions
- stimulate the flow of the universal life force through your body and energy field
- learn to experience your consciousness outside of your head, or thoughts
- learn how to move your consciousness around
- stimulate the psychic faculty

Before you undertake this exercise, familiarize yourself with the location and names of the primary chakras.

Sit in a comfortable chair, relaxed with your spine straight. Relax with Psychic Power Breathing.

Close your eyes and imagine yourself to be a ball of white light. All of your consciousness is centered in this light.

Move the light to the root chakra at the base of the spine. Feel the light pulsing there. Breathe into the light and into the root chakra for a minute or two.

Imagine that the light is on a string and you can pull it up. Pull the light into the second chakra, the spleen, located under the navel and to the left. Breathe into the light and the spleen chakra for a minute or two.

Then pull the light up into the third chakra, the solar plexus, located just below the navel. Feel the light pulsing there and breathe into the light and the chakra.

Continue on up the chakras, moving next to:

- the heart chakra in the center of the chest
- the throat chakra at the base of the throat
- the third eye chakra between and slightly above the brows
- the crown chakra at the top of the head

When you reach the crown, allow the light to cascade down around you so that you are enveloped in it. The crown chakra is the seat of spiritual and mystical enlightenment, and integration of the whole self.

As you go through this exercise, you may notice that it is difficult, perhaps to leave certain chakras. If you feel resistance to pulling the light up, stay in that chakra. Visualize the light bathing the chakra in a soothing fashion. Move up only when you feel you can pull the light up. Your consciousness may be intuitively drawn to stay in a chakra because energy there needs to be stimulated.

Spend about twenty minutes on this exercise. If you only get through two or three chakras, that is fine. Pay attention to the intuitive impressions around each chakra.

For a variation on this exercise, change the color of the light to match each chakra:

- Root – red

- Spleen – orange
- Solar plexus – yellow
- Heart – green
- Throat – blue
- Third eye – indigo
- Crown – violet

    This exercise is also called chakra clearing. Energy in the chakras can become blocked or sluggish due to physical, emotional and spiritual factors. Repressed emotions from our experiences can adversely affect the chakra energy as well. In esoteric thought, moving energy through them helps them to function better, and thus benefit our physical, mental, emotional and spiritual health. When you're in optimum health, your psychic ability functions better, too.

Key #4

Ball of Light

Psychic ability is nonlocal and operates independently of time and space. To give it freer rein, we must expand the experiences of our own consciousness.

When asked to pinpoint the location of consciousness, most people say the head or the brain. We associate our thoughts and feelings with the brain, and therefore what we are, our sum awareness, must be in the head.

In order to be intuitive and psychic, you have to get out of the head, and become comfortable with the idea that consciousness is not limited to the body. The psychic side of us knows, sees and understands things that are beyond reach of the physical senses.

Whether you are aware of it or not, your consciousness travels all the time. It travels in the dreams of sleep, in the daydreams of reverie, in flashes of insight or inspiration, in mutual moments of "Oh, I was just thinking about you!" and whenever the intuitive/psychic faculty functions.

The purpose of the Ball of Light exercises is to expand the boundaries of your self-awareness, the map you carry of the world of your consciousness. You can do them by yourself.

Exercise #1: Traveling Around the Body

Center yourself and relax with Psychic Power Breathing.

Close your eyes and imagine yourself to be a ball of white light. All of your consciousness is centered in this light. Start with the light located in your head, where most of us identify the seat of consciousness. Fill your head with light. Feel its warmth. Spend a few minutes experiencing what it is like to be a ball of light inside the head. Perhaps you will see your brain lit from within.

Now move your light down into your heart. Feel your entire chest fill with light. What is it like to be centered in your heart?

Go down into your stomach. What do you see? What you do feel? Can you experience your own digestion? Do any thoughts or emotions arise from your stomach? If your stomach could talk, what would it tell you?

Move your light up into the throat. Spend a few minutes there, experiencing what the throat is, and what it has to tell you.

Move your light around your body. To your foot. Your hand. Various organs. The blood. Your bones.

Bring your light to back to your heart. This is where your soul connection to the Source lies. To be intuitive and psychic, you must be heart-centered and not head-centered. The heart-centered person is open to exploration and is in touch with feelings and sensations. Allow your light to bathe and fill your heart. Send rays of light radiating out into the world. The rays of light are your consciousness and your soul essence, pouring forth in an eternal stream, connecting you to everything else in the cosmos. Feel the connection, like links in a web. Everything is interwoven. You are part of the Web of All Things.

Recenter yourself in your body with Psychic Power Breathing.

Record your experience in your journal.

Exercise #2: Expanding Your Consciousness

Center yourself and relax with Psychic Power Breathing.

Close your eyes and imagine yourself to be a ball of white light. Place your light in the solar plexus chakra, just below the navel. The solar plexus, like the heart, maintains an important link to the Web of All Things upon which psychic power travels.

Feel your light fill the solar plexus. Experience its warmth.

Contract your light. Make it very small. The size of a baseball... a ping pong ball... a pea. Make it infinitesimally small, so small the physical eye cannot see it. But the intuitive eye can.

Now make your light grow in size. It becomes bigger than a baseball. Allow it to keep growing. It extends beyond the solar plexus. It extends out from the body. Keep expanding the light until it becomes bigger than the body, and envelopes the body in it.

Push the light out and out. Fill the room you are in. Move beyond the room. Fill the house or building you are in.

There are no limits to your light, just as there are no limits to your consciousness. You are the light. Keep expanding. Fill your city, your country, the planet. Extend into space. What do you experience?

Gradually contract your light. Recenter your consciousness in your body with Psychic Power Breathing.

Record your experience in your journal.

Exercise #3: Traveling Beyond the Body

Center yourself and relax with Psychic Power Breathing.

Close your eyes and imagine yourself to be a ball of white light. Center your light comfortably within the body. Imagine that your light has become a balloon and can float upward. Float up to the ceiling in the room. Without looking at it with your physical eyes, "see" the detail of the ceiling and "feel" its texture. If this seems difficult, remind yourself that all of your senses have come with you in the light. It's perfectly natural and very easy for you to experience with your unlimited senses.

Now make your light grow heavy and descend to the floor. Again, without opening your physical eyes, see and feel the floor.

Bring your light up and move it around the room, keeping your eyes closed. Move into a corner. What do you experience? Look under a piece of furniture, cabinet or table. What do you see?

Now move your light out of the room. Go into a hallway or adjacent room. Explore that area. Allow impressions to arise naturally. Do not worry about being accurate. Do not try to create impressions from memory of what you might know.

Return your light to your room and to your body. Recenter your light within your body with Psychic Power Breathing.

Check the accuracy of your impressions.

Record your experience in your journal.

Do these different exercises frequently. Choose one each day for a week. They are building blocks for the more advanced exercises that follow in this book.

In Exercise 3, Traveling Beyond the Body, you can travel as far away as you want. However, it may then be impossible to verify the accuracy of your impressions. For best results, try places that you can easily visit to inspect later.

Key #5

Expanded Vision

When I visited Japan, I had the pleasure of attending tea ceremony classes taught by The Little Tea Society in Tokyo. My enjoyment of these classes led to further study of the history and ritual of tea. Japanese tea ceremony is both art form and spiritual path, and some of the fundamental elements in it pertain to psychic power.

In developing psychic power, you first learn to train consciousness to hold a steady focus, and to expand sensory awareness to pick up subtle and extrasensory cues and information. So it is with tea ceremony. Everything in the ceremony is precise: the selection and arrangement of utensils; the arrangement and decorations of the tea room; the clothing worn; the order in which the ceremony is done. Server and participants have precise roles to play in what they do and say. All of this requires concentration and mindfulness. When you are doing tea, you are fully in the ceremony. Nothing else matters. The rest of the world recedes. Every bit of your attention and sensory awareness is focused.

Tea ceremony contains quite a bit of mystery. In fact, it is more than ceremony—it is *chado*, or "the way of tea." *Chanoyu*, or tea ceremony itself, arose in fifteenth-century Japan. It embodies the philosophy and rituals of Buddhism, Taoism and Zen. Schools of tea arose and created tea masters who devoted their lives to perfecting the mystery of *chanoyu*. By practicing *chanoyu*, one unfolds spiritually.

In tea, one pays careful attention to the senses. When the student enters the tea room, he devotes time to looking at it, appreciating its beauty. He listens to the sound of the water boiling in the tea kettle. He absorbs aromas and savors tastes. When the tea is served, he looks at the serving bowl, noticing its colors, texture and artistry. He examines the tea utensils and containers. His careful observation enables him to see ordinary objects as extraordinary. It is a precious moment of eternity, never to be repeated.

In these exercises, we will focus our sense of sight as though we were students of tea. We will experience with the knowledge that we will never be in the same moment again. Thus, we will appreciate fully each moment.

Exercise #1: Zen Viewing

Go around your home and select five objects at random from any room. Five is the number of change, especially spiritual change. Thus it is the number of the intuition and psychic power, for using psychic power brings change.

Arrange the objects in a row in front of you. Center yourself with Psychic Power Breathing and relaxation. Contemplate your objects. Gaze at them one by one and as a group. One by one, pick up each object and give it your full attention. Observe colors, textures, imperfections, symmetry. Look at it as though you were seeing it for the first and last time in your life. Think about its origin and its purpose, who made it, its usefulness and its place in your home. Record your impressions and thoughts for each object.

Do this exercise three times a week. What changes do you notice in how you look at things? Do you have a new and different appreciation of detail? Do you observe details that you did not before? Do you have a new and different appreciation about the objects themselves? How do these changes extend to the world beyond your home?

Exercise #2: Appreciating Art

Art is a manifestation of beauty, and when you contemplate beauty, you raise your spiritual consciousness and open the gateway to psychic power. Art is everywhere, of course, but museums and galleries offer places to find concentrations of it. Yet how many times have you strolled through a museum and really looked at the art as you walked by it?

In the East, appreciation of art is part of one's holistic spiritual path. Art speaks to the intuition in a direct way that bypasses words and linear thought.

Okakura Tenshin, who wrote the classic book about Japanese tea ceremony, *The Book of Tea*, had this to say about the effect of art upon consciousness:

> Nothing is more hallowing than the union of kindred spirits in art. At the moment of meeting, the art lover transcends himself. At once he is and is not. He catches a glimpse of Infinity, but words cannot voice his delight, for the eye has no tongue. Freed from the fetters of matter, his spirit moves in the rhythm of things. It is thus that art becomes akin to religion and ennobles mankind. It is this which makes a masterpiece sacred.

For this exercise, visit a museum or art gallery. Select five works of art of any kind—painting, sculpture, pottery, artifact—and study each one as you did with your home objects. You will not be able to touch or handle these, of course.

Immerse yourself in the minute details of each work. Contemplate the origin, purpose, and creator. If the artist is not known, allow your intuition to fill in the answer. What does each work of art have to say to you? What stories does it have to tell? Does it transport you to another time? What attracted you to this particular object?

The spirit, or consciousness, of the artist lives on in the work. Attune yourself to this spirit. What can your intuition tell you about the artist and his or her inspiration?

Record your experiences and thoughts.

Exercise #3: Appreciating God's Art

Now turn your attention to the art gallery of nature. Choose a spot outdoors. It can be your backyard, a park, or a more exotic locale.

Prepare yourself as for meditation, with Psychic Power Breathing and relaxation. Select five objects at random, near or distant: flowers, bushes, trees, stones, clouds, hills, or whatever draws your attention. It might also be an animal, such as a squirrel foraging for food.

Observe each in as much detail as possible, as though you are seeing it for the first and last time in your life. What drew you to your choices? What messages do they have for you? In the lore of angels, it is said that there is an angel to watch over everything in nature, including every blade of grass. Ask the angels of your choices to speak to you. Imagine a line of white and gold light extending from your heart to the heart of each thing you selected. Feel this connection. Now extend the connection to all of nature.

What do you experience? Record your thoughts and impressions.

One of the benefits of these exercises, besides strengthening psychic power, is to increase awareness of the indwelling spirit, or immanence, of God in all things. The divine spark is in everything in the world of nature, in all creatures, plants, stones and geophysical features. The divine spark is manifest in whatever human beings create, including works of art and everyday objects intended to benefit daily life.

The awareness of this immanence makes the presence of God tangible. It puts us into direct contact with the power of creation. We not only see things differently, we see life differently. And, we live life differently-more fully, more abundantly.

Exercise #4: Reading Body Language

Your expanded vision can be directed at the body language signals given by others. Our bodies express what we're *really* feeling or thinking. Psychics pay attention to detail, and detail reveals a great deal of information. There are obvious body language signals that most of us know. For example, crossed arms and or legs often indicate defensiveness.

Many body language signals are subtle. When you talk to others, listen with your eyes as well as your ears. What is communicated to you intuitively? How well does body language match what is being said?

You may want to study literature on body language, but do not allow it to set preconceived ideas for you. Be open to what your intuition tells you from your own observations.

Key #6

Expanded Listening

The skilled psychic learns to hear with the inner ear as well as the outer ear. In these exercises, you will extend your physical sense of hearing to pick up on the subtle sounds and cues of the world around us, and on the inner plane.

The practice of Expanded Listening will help you to develop an entirely new sense of hearing. Mystics experience this spiritual, or soul, hearing. According to Rudolph Steiner, all higher truths are obtained only through the disciplined use of senses to experience inner promptings:

> The soul becomes capable of hearing "words" from the spiritual world that are not expressed in outer tones and cannot be heard by physical ears. Perception of the "inner world" awakens. Truths are gradually revealed to us out of the spiritual world. We hear ourselves spoken to spiritually.

Intuition flows from the higher truths or Truth.

Exercise #1: Sounds of the Outer Environment

In your own home, settle into a comfortable spot and enter a meditative state with your eyes closed. Allow the silence to thicken around you. Listen to the sounds of the environment around you: cars passing by on the street, airplanes flying overhead, birds singing outside, appliances humming, and so on. Experience each sound fully. Allow it to pass through you.

Now imagine that your ears are extremely sensitive antennae. Extend your listening out farther and farther into physical space. Can you hear the sounds of a highway some distance away? The sound of an appliance in another part of the house? The sounds of the airport twenty miles away? The sound of a river one hundred miles away? The sound of the ocean two hundred miles away? The sounds of a city 1000 miles away? And so on. Keep pushing out the boundaries of what you can hear. There are no limits. Become immersed in the sounds.

After you end the exercise, record your experiences.

As a variation, you can start this exercise out-of-doors and focus on the sounds of nature. Hear the obvious sounds. Then, as you extend your sensitivity, listen for the softer and more subtle sounds of nature: the rustling of small animals and birds in bushes, leaves rustling in trees, insects crawling through blades of grass, the sound of clouds moving through the sky, the sound of things growing.

Record your experiences.

Exercise #2: Sounds of the Inner Environment

Enter into a meditative state with your eyes closed. Become aware of the sounds of your environment. Allow them to pass through you.

Now turn your attention inward. Listen carefully to the sound of your breathing. Become totally immersed in the sound.

Go deeper. Hear your heartbeat. Listen to your digestion. Then go deeper still to hear the blood rushing through the veins and arteries. Go deeper still. Hear the sounds of cells doing their jobs to keep your physical house functioning. Listen for the impulses of brain activity.

Go deeper still, deep into the interior of your being, where you hear the sound of the cosmic currents of being.

Record your experiences. Did any sounds surprise you?

The psychic sense often speaks through subtle environmental cues. Do these exercises often to sharpen your listening skills. Affirm to yourself, *"I hear Truth."*

Make note of any other psychic information that comes as a result of expanded listening: messages, information, ideas and so on.

The more you develop your inner hearing, the more selective you will become about what you hear. Background sound and noise that once seemed necessary to you, such as a radio or television set going constantly, will become less desirable. Discordant sound and the sound of violence, such as that present in much popular music, film and TV shows, will also become less desirable. You will find yourself naturally preferring silence or sounds that are pleasing and harmonious.

Perhaps one of your experiences of Expanded Listening will be to hear the sound of creation. Primordial sound, as it is called in mystical traditions, is sound beyond sound. From primordial sound come the sounds of divinity as expressed in all the names of God.

Our spiritual health—and therefore our psychic health—is governed by the diet we feed it. Our diet consists of not only the food we eat, but also what we eat with our ears and our eyes.

Key #7

Riding the Waves

All things in the universe are composed of energy. The energy can assume any form, and can become organized into patterns, such as the physical realm. Matter is energy. Consciousness is energy. Our thoughts and feelings are energy. Creativity is energy. Psychic ability is energy. The essence of the soul is energy.

The energies of the universe are in constant motion and interplay. As energies affect each other, they change form. In this exercise, we will change the form of our energy, transmuting the body, which has limitations, into waves of energy, which have no limit. As a wave of energy, you can travel wherever you need to go to tap into your intuition.

For Riding the Waves, imagine yourself at the seashore. Stand with bare feet at the water's edge. Watch the waves roll in and lap the beach. Smell the salt air. Feel the crunch of the sand beneath your feet. Hear the sound of the waves, the cries of shore birds. The ocean stretches into infinity.

Notice that the sunlight falling upon the water makes the surface sparkle like millions of gems. You are warm, happy and content. You are fully present to the moment. There is no past, no tomorrow, only the eternal moment.

Focus your attention on the action of the waves. The water rolls in, the water rolls out. Timeless, eternal motion.

Imagine that your consciousness flows out from you in waves of energy. See the waves rippling from you. Synchronize the waves of your consciousness with the ocean waves. Let yourself become lighter and lighter. Your body changes into waves of energy. Become lighter still, until you are only energy. Flow out over the ocean waves.

Now you are a wave of energy riding along the waves of the ocean. Feel the flow, the surge and ebb. The tide is going out. Allow yourself to be carried along with it, easily, gently. You are filled with complete peace and harmony, at one with the sparkling ocean. You feel energized. The ocean is the universe. You are one with the currents of the universe.

The currents carry you out and out. Here you are free of distraction. Here you are free of limitation. You can know the answers to all questions. You can know all things.

A message is given to you. Perhaps the ocean speaks it. Perhaps a bird cries it. Perhaps the clouds write it across the sky. Perhaps it wells up within you as something you knew all along.

Give thanks for your message. Know that it is right for you.

When you feel ready, return to awareness of your physical body.

Record your experience. What impressions did you have of what "you" were like in form?

Riding the Waves will help you become comfortable with operation of your psychic power as an ability not limited by your body.

Key #8

Remote Viewing

In Expanded Vision (Key #5), you learned to focus your vision on detail and subtle cues. Now you will work with your inner vision, and send it to hidden and distant locations. The traditional term for this is clairvoyance, and a modern term is "remote viewing." It is a psychic/intuitive skill known and used since ancient times. The term "remote viewing" was coined in the 1970s by American physicists Russell Targ and Harold Puthoff, who researched the phenomenon of seeing at a distance. Targ also called it "remote sensing," since impressions of smell, sound, and touch are part of the experience.

Historically, remote viewing has been associated with psychically gifted and trained persons such as oracles, shamans, magical adepts, and mediums. The faculty of remote viewing is one of the *siddhis* described in the *Yoga Sutras* written by Patanjali about 3000 years ago. The *siddhis* are paranormal or extraordinary powers attained through spiritual development, such as through various paths of yoga. *Siddhis* means "perfect abilities" or "miraculous powers." They include clairvoyance, telepathy, mind-reading, levitation, materialization, invisibility, superhuman strength, knowledge of one's death, and the ability to project out of one's own body and into another's body. The *siddhis* should not be sought for themselves. Rather, they arise as a natural part of spiritual advancement. If one gets caught up in their enchantment, one stops spiritual advancement.

In the late eighteenth and early nineteenth centuries, hypnotists observed that ordinary people, when hypnotized, often could give detailed accounts of distant locations. Not only could they describe surroundings, people, clothing and activities, some could "see" into distant stomachs to report their contents, and "see" into brains. Meanwhile, mediums popularized public performances of "billet reading," in which they "read" messages in sealed envelopes with eyes closed or while blindfolded. Psychical researchers conducted many controlled scientific experiments with blindfolded subjects.

Targ and Putoff, using more sophisticated modern methodologies, collected impressive results in their experiments of remote viewing at SRI International, formerly Stanford Research Institute. They concluded that remote viewing is a psychic experience that occurs naturally in the lives of many people. They found they could train others to remote view, regardless of their natural psychic ability and previous psychic experiences or training.

Most remote viewers can be taught to go to a location and accurately describe buildings, geographic features, people and activities. In many cases, the further away the target, the greater the accuracy. They also can be taught to see into opaque containers to describe contents (the modern version of billet reading), and to read data and see images on microdot film.

The U.S. government became interested in remote viewing, and financed research into the possible uses of it for intelligence gathering, warfare and espionage. Viewers were given intensive training. Typically, they were asked to describe distant locations knowing only the latitude and longitude as reference points. Overall, the government's success in psychic espionage was mixed, perhaps for reasons elaborated below.

Once rather exotic, remote viewing classes and training are now readily available to the general public. There is nothing difficult or tricky about it—anyone can learn to send consciousness traveling to a distant or physically inaccessible spot. With training and practice come increasing accuracy.

Remote viewing has various practical applications. Remote viewers are used to survey distant sites. They are flown over terrain to sense hidden water sources and mineral, gem, coal, and gas deposits. Psychics who work with police on crime solving use remote viewing to locate missing persons or bodies. Remote viewing can look into the past to recreate a crime victim's last activities and movements. Looking into the past (retrocognition) may be of use in archaeology. Remote viewers can also look into the future. Several of the Keys in this section utilize remote viewing in different ways.

A word about ethics: Some people are drawn to remote viewing training because they think it will enable them to spy upon others. In the mystical traditions, the misuse of the power of the *siddhis* boomerangs back upon the user, ultimately affecting overall health. Remote viewers have found that people who do not wish their privacy of place or person invaded will not be open to invasion. And, they find that the continued use of remote viewing for selfish purposes drains one's vitality—literally the life force. The higher powers respond to higher spiritual laws. When you undertake remote viewing, it must be for the purposes of help and healing, not for entertainment.

Exercise #1: Place Viewing

For this exercise, you will need a partner. Decide who will be the tester and who will be the subject. In advance, the tester will select five images of places and place them inside opaque, sealed envelopes. The images can be photos, drawings, or pictures clipped from magazines. They can be cityscapes, nature vistas, buildings, and so on. They must be *places*. Number the envelopes and make a record of the contents of each envelope.

Arrange a time to get together with your partner, the subject. Place sealed envelope #1 in front of the subject. The subject has fifteen minutes to "see" the image inside. The subject should write down his or her impressions, including any drawings. The subject is not allowed to handle the envelope.

When the first envelope is done, continue through the remaining four, one by one. At the completion, open the envelopes one by one and see how well the subject did.

The subject's impressions may be generalized. For example, you may see geometric impressions and not specific landscape features. Straight lines may be tall buildings.

Do this exercise regularly, switching roles and shortening the time the subject has to receive and record impressions to five minutes. Are you more accurate with less time? Sometimes, the more time we have to think about our impressions, the less accurate we are, because we make judgments on what we receive.

Exercise #2: People Viewing

Make arrangements with a friend or family member that you will look in on them by remote viewing at an appointed time. Select a time during which the other party—your target—knows where he will be. For example, at 8 PM, he will be at home. At 10 AM, he will be in the office. These are places with which you should have at least some familiarity: you have seen the home, and know at least something general about the office (such as its location downtown, for example). Ascertain only the place where the target will be; do not collect any information about what your target will be doing.

Prepare yourself as for meditation with Psychic Power Breathing and relaxation. Close your eyes. Think of the target and call up a vivid visual impression and name. Visualize them where they are in as much detail as possible. At first this will seem like an exercise of imagination, but your expanded senses will take over quickly.

Release any expectations you have of what the target *should* be doing. You must be open and neutral to whatever impressions arise. Pretend you are watching a movie—you don't know what's going to happen next. Do not judge or analyze any impressions, which will immediately interfere with the process. For example, if a piece of furniture seems out of place, do not question its location—it may have been moved.

Can you picture your target clearly? What is he doing? What details in the surroundings do you notice? Do you receive any emotional impressions? Do you notice any sounds or smells? Do you feel any sensations of heat or cold? Are there other people in your remote viewing movie?

Record your impressions, no matter how sketchy. You may not experience anything like a movie, but instead receive fragments of impressions. Do not disregard anything.

Key #8 | Remote Viewing

Later, check with your target. How well do your impressions match what really transpired?

Repeat the exercise. The more you practice it, the better results you will obtain. You will notice more detail.

Variations of remote viewing are presented in Key #17, Hide and Seek.

Key #9

Reading Objects and Photographs

Everyday objects are repositories of information accessible by psychic skill. Sound impossible? It's actually an age-old, world-wide belief, one that has been borne out by experience. Obtaining information from objects is called psychometry, from the Greek words *psyche* (the soul) and *metron* (measure). There is no scientific basis for psychometry, but it works. I have used psychometry for years. Now is your chance to test your own psychometry ability. Consider it your "expanded touch."

The idea behind psychometry is that objects retain an energy imprint of people who own and handle them over a period of time. If an intuitive person holds the object and "tunes in," impressions about the owner(s) will arise.

Psychometry has an interesting history. The word "psychometry" was coined in 1840 by Joseph R. Buchanan, an American professor of physiology who saw psychometry as a means to measure the "soul" of objects and "grasp and estimate all things which are within range of human intelligence." Buchanan conducted experiments in which students could identify drugs in vials by holding the vials. He kept his research quiet for nine years out of fear of ridicule.

Buchanan's work interested Professor William F. Denton, an American professor of geology, who conducted his own experiments in 1854 with his sister, Ann Denton Cridge. When Cridge placed wrapped geological specimen to her forehead, she experienced vivid mental images of their appearances. Denton, who did not consider the possibility of telepathy between himself and his sister, recorded his experiments in a book, *The Soul of Things*. He defined psychometry as a "mysterious faculty which belongs to the soul and is not dependent upon the body for its exercise."

Psychometry was popularized by mediums, who "read" the contents of sealed letters. Today psychometry is used in psychic criminology and psychic archaeology. In psychic criminology, psychics handle a personal object belonging to or associated with a crime victim or missing person in order to get clues that will help solve the crime or locate the person or body. Objects worn during stress, especially the trauma of crime, convey the most vivid impressions. In psychic archaeology, psychics receive impressions from artifacts to identify their uses and historical dates. Even stones and bricks yield data.

I have used psychometry for years in doing psychic readings. For example, when I hold someone's watch or ring, I impressions in the form of images, words and feelings.

Everyone interested in psychic development should try psychometry. You'll probably be surprised at what you can do with it.

Exercise #1: Reading Objects

For this exercise, work with a partner, ideally someone you do not know well or at all. You will need a small personal possession and notepad and pen. Preferably, your possession should be made of metal, as metal seems to retain the strongest impressions. Jewelry, watches, cosmetics cases, keys, and keychains all can do quite nicely. For best results, the object should belong only to the wearer and should have been in possession for at least three months. Gifts from others are fine, but avoid such things as antique or secondhand jewelry, or jewelry handed down through families. The objects will have the energy imprints of all their owners, and thus you will receive confusing or muddy intuitive impressions.

Exchange objects with your partner. Each of you close your eyes and hold the object. Pay attention to the spontaneous words, images, and thoughts that arise to your inner mind and eye. Do not disregard or discard anything, no matter how incongruous or "inappropriate" it seems. Do not evaluate or judge; just pay attention.

Continuing with your eyes closed, examine your object for five minutes without speaking. Then look at it with open eyes. Jot down notes about your impressions and any associations with them, so that you don't forget anything. You may be flooded with impressions. Or, you may receive only one or two. Don't be frustrated if you receive very little—sometimes a single, small impression unlocks a wealth of insight. Don't try to force more. Your expectations, fear of failure, and imagination will interfere.

When the five minutes is up, take turns sharing your impressions. Do not provide any feedback until the other person is done speaking about you. If you don't know what an impression means, just say so. Most likely, you will have an intuitive feel for what an impression conveys.

For example, in a reading for a young man, I had a vivid image of a horse racetrack while I held his watch. The empty track was muddy and pounded, as though many horses had gone over it. What could that mean? Did he like to go to the races? Did he own a race horse? Was he in a race against time? The psychic feeling that accompanied this image said otherwise. I felt that he was stressed by competition. He wasn't one of the horses or jockeys, however (note that my impression featured neither of those). He was the racetrack, and that's how he felt—pounded. Furthermore, I had the feeling that this did not relate to work, which would have been the logical assumption, but to family. All of these impressions and more arose simultaneously in my mind while I held the watch.

I described the image to him and said, "I have the feeling that you experience a lot of competition for attention in your family, and that you're in a race to be the first or the best. This is the way it's always been, and you're tired of it. It has drained a lot of your energy, especially your emotional energy, and it's not getting you anywhere—you just keep going around in circles. It's somebody else's race, not yours. Deep inside, you'd like to quit it."

It was all right on target. The young man was struggling with a desire to pursue his own interests in life rather than fulfill the expectations of a competitive family. The image of the empty and pounded track was a powerful one for him, validating his true feelings.

Another time, as I held a woman's ring, I saw a tennis ball bouncing back and forth across a net. No players or racquets, just a ball going from this side to that. It turned out that the woman was in the middle of a family dispute, and was being bounced from one side to the other. The dispute was more a "game" between two family members who were both using her. She was able to extricate herself from the situation without guilt.

Not all impressions are going to deal with major matters. For example, you may see an image of a house filled with vases of lovely flowers, and then learn that the other person loves to garden and keeps her house filled with cut blossoms.

Try a new partner. This time, hold the objects for one minute instead of five. Then describe your impressions and associations.

Try another new partner. You will not need your notepads or pens, but will work alternately, one at a time. Take your partner's object, hold it and begin speaking immediately. When you are done, let your partner give feedback. Switch roles.

This progression of faster and faster responses will help you train your psychic awareness to be rapid and fluid. Also, you will not have time to stop and evaluate what you are receiving, so you are less likely to let left-brain judgement interfere. Intuition arises quickly.

Exercise #2: Reading Hidden Objects

For more challenge, wrap your object and seal it inside a plain white envelope or a box. In the exercise, handle only the sealed envelope or box. You may or may not be able to guess what the object is, but you will not have unconscious associations that can arise from seeing it, such as "This is an expensive watch, so he must be affluent," or "This is an odd ring, so she must like unusual things."

Follow the procedures outlined in Exercise 1.

Exercise #3: Reading Photographs

Is a photograph a lifeless image, or does it contain a spark of a person's essence, soul, or spirit? Many peoples around the world believe that a photograph captures the soul, and therefore do not like to have their photos taken, especially by strangers.

There's some truth in that belief. A photograph may not actually steal your soul, but it does carry your essence, and it can be psychometrized like your personal possessions and your aura. Now that you have gained some familiarity with psychometry, try your skill on photographs.

Select two photos from your personal collection: one of you and one of a family member or friend who is living. For best results, the photos should be recent. Current information can be obtained from old photographs, but may be obscured by old information.

Work with a partner who also has selected two photographs. Neither of you shares any information about the photos, when or where they were taken, or the identities of the other persons. Exchange the photos of yourselves. Spend three minutes examining them and recording your impressions. Try to see beyond the photos themselves. Experiment with averted vision. Hold the palm of one hand over the photo. Don't be surprised if the photo seems to come "alive." Perhaps the image will talk to you. Perhaps you will see objects or places in the space around the photograph. You may receive impressions of emotions, or of events that have happened to the person.

When the time is up, set those photos aside and take the second photos. Do the same, spending three minutes reading them.

When the reading period is finished, share your psychic impressions about both photographs. Wait for your partner to give all impressions on both photos before offering any feedback.

How did you do? Were you able to correctly identify the second person? Or perhaps you saw something, such as an activity, that linked that person to your partner. Were your impressions predominantly emotional in tone? Or did you see mostly events? A mixture? Were any of your impressions precognitive, relating to possible future events?

How did you feel about photographs compared to your psychometry practice with objects?

If you don't feel "in the flow" after repeated practice with psychometry, don't worry. It doesn't mean you are not psychic. Everyone has resonances with different techniques.

Key #10

Reading Auras

A person's aura can be psychometrized just like an object. To a clairvoyant, the envelope of energy around someone contains a wealth of physical, mental, emotional, and spiritual information about them.

Whether you're aware of it or not, you read an aura whenever you meet someone. We all have first impressions that we cannot ascribe to known facts. People make us feel at ease or ill at ease; we sense sadness around them even when their demeanor is happy, and so on. We are picking up psychic cues from the energy field around a person.

This exercise is similar to psychometry with objects; familiarize yourself with Key #9 first.

Exercise #1: Reading Auras with Touch

On straight-backed chairs, sit facing a partner. Decide which of you will read first.

Relax and center with Psychic Power Breathing. Imagine that the two of you are enveloped in a bubble of white light. The white light wraps you in a loving energy. Send loving thoughts to your partner, wishing that whatever comes from the exercise will be of benefit to them.

When you feel ready, hold out your hands palms up. Your partner will place his or her hands palm down on top of yours. Through this connection, you are tapped in to the energy of your partner's aura. Allow your psychic impressions to arise spontaneously within you. You can keep your eyes closed or open. You are likely to feel more comfortable with them closed. Allow your mind to float and stay detached from results.

Hold the connection for three minutes. You can rest your hands on your lap. When the time is up, thank your partner and share your impressions. Receive feedback. Then switch roles.

Like the Reading Objects exercise, this one also progresses in speed. Change partners and do it again, spending only one minute tuning in through the hands, then share your impressions and get feedback. Switch roles.

Change partners again, and this time begin speaking as soon as you connect through the hands.

The first times you try this exercise, you may freeze up under the pressure of performing in a short period of time. Relax and keep trying. Remember that the more relaxed you are, the more successful you will be. Don't be concerned about how much material you can produce. None of these exercises is a contest. Trust that you will receive what will be of help to your partner. That may be a lot of information, or just a single impression.

Exercise #2: Reading Auras without Touch

Try this series again but without any physical contact with your partner. Sit facing him or her. Imagine the white bubble of loving energy around the two of you, send loving thoughts, and ask to be of help. Then allow your impressions to arise.

Did you notice a difference in using touch versus not touching? Was one method more productive for you? For some, even a slight contact facilitates the flow of impressions, rather like holding a metal object.

Even if you felt you got more from touching, practice this exercise frequently without touch. In real-life application, it is not always feasible or advisable to touch others. These different techniques will teach you the subtleties of your own intuition. Ultimately, you will feel confident about tapping into your intuition anytime and anywhere.

Key #11

Pendulum Dowsing

The pendulum is a popular tool for activating the psychic sense. It has been used for thousands of years in dowsing, which is a form of divination for locating lost and missing persons and animals, detecting hidden objects and substances, such as water, oil, coal, minerals, cables and pipes, and obtaining information. Dowsing also is used in the mapping of archaeological sites. Many people dowse about decisions and choices for virtually any purpose. Paranormal investigators use dowsing to communicate with discarnate beings, and to map unusual energy fields and lines in haunted locations.

No one knows exactly how or why dowsing works. The dowsing tool responds to the user. For example, if a dowser is looking for underground water with L-shaped rods, the rods will signal where the water is by moving up and down or back and forth. A pendulum will whirl. Along with the signals from the tool, the dowser may also get psychic impressions. Dowsers do not necessarily need to go on location to search for things. Many dowse maps in a type of remote viewing.

Dowsing is at least 7000 years old, and its exact origins are unknown. Ancient Egyptian art portrays dowsers with forked rods and headdresses with antennae. Ancient Chinese kings used dowsing rods. The Kalahari bushmen of Africa have long used dowsing to find sources of water.

During the Middle Ages, dowsing was used widely in Europe and Great Britain to locate underground water and coal deposits. It was associated with the supernatural, which gave rise to the terms "water witching" and "wizard's rod." Among the first books on the subject were *The Diviners* by Gaspard Peucer, published in 1553 and *De Re Metallica* by Agricola, published in 1556 in Germany. Dowsing was transplanted to America by the early colonists.

Dowsing was widely used until the nineteenth century, when scientists dismissed it as superstition. In the twentieth century, dowsing made a comeback as a psychic skill, especially in Europe and Great Britain, where it has been successfully used in archaeological digs, the search for minerals, and in medicine. During war time, dowsers helped locate mines, unexploded shells and buried mortars for the military.

In the United States, dowsing is used by some oil, gas and minerals companies, who have found dowsers to be often more accurate than geologists using scientific techniques. Many water and pipe companies use dowsing to locate buried cables and pipes find damaged spots. In the Vietnam War, the Marines used dowsing rods to locate mines, booby traps and sunken mortar shells. Dowsers also have contributed research towards the understanding of mysterious earth energies, such as ley lines.

The pendulum has become the dowsing tool of choice over rods, perhaps due to its small size and convenience. It can be easily kept in a pocket or pouch. Some pendulums can be quite fancy and expensive, made out of sterling silver chains and carved crystals or precious stones. Others are less elegant and costly but are equally effective. The pendulum is an excellent tool for focusing your psychic sense.

Exercise #1: Training the Pendulum

First you must train the pendulum to say yes and no. Center yourself with Psychic Power Breathing to achieve a relaxed and tranquil mind. Hold the pendulum steady and ask, "Give me a yes." Do not try to stimulate movement. Allow it to respond naturally. After a few moments, the pendulum will begin to rotate or swing back and forth. The more vigorous the motion, the stronger the response. Stop the pendulum and hold it steady again. Ask, "Give me a no." Allow the pendulum to respond naturally again.

Most likely, the no will be the opposite motion of the yes. If the pendulum rotates clockwise for yes, it probably will rotate counterclockwise for no.

Ask the pendulum a series of yes and no questions to which you know the answers. "Is my name John Doe?" "Do I live at 47 Jackson Street?" and so on. With each question, allow the pendulum to respond of its own accord. If it remains motionless, ask the question again.

Then ask questions that have emotional intensity behind them—something you feel strongly about that can be worded in a yes or no way. Does your pendulum respond more vigorously?

Work with your pendulum every day by asking it obvious questions. Trust the pendulum to reflect your psychic sense.

Exercise #2: Yes and No

Once you feel comfortable working with your pendulum, use it daily to answer yes or no questions. Start with simple things, such as a route to work, an activity, an errand, etc. If you start with major issues, you may be nervous about the results and have difficulty accepting the answers.

If you ask a question and the pendulum does not respond, it may mean neutrality.

When you feel secure in trusting the response of the pendulum, gradually increase the importance of questions.

You can also consult the pendulum for timing. Keep in mind that questions need to be framed in a yes-or-no context. For example, if you are contemplating a move, you can ask questions like, "Would spring be a good time to move?" or "Would next month be a good time to move?"

Look for ways to validate the answers. Perhaps something worked out well in your favor, or you avoided an inconvenience. Notice any corresponding psychic signals from your body, senses or impressions that arise in the mind.

Exercise #3: Lost and Found

For this exercise, you will need a partner. One of you will hide an object; the other will find it with pendulum dowsing.

First, an object known to both parties will be hidden indoors, such as in a person's home. The seeker will search for it with the pendulum.

Visualize the object as vividly as possible in your mind. Give verbal instructions to the pendulum to alert you to its location. Hold the pendulum steady and then walk around the site. When the pendulum starts to move in an affirmative manner, such as swinging in clockwise circles, you know you are close. The closer you are, the more the pendulum should move.

Try this exercise out of doors.

In a more difficult variation, an object unknown to the seeker is hidden indoors. You, the seeker, cannot visualize it, but you can ask the pendulum to locate the hidden object and reveal its identity. Follow the movements of the pendulum. The closer you are, the more the pendulum will move. The object may be truly hidden from sight, or may be in plain view.

Do this variation of the exercise out of doors.

In all cases, note how long it takes you to locate the target object. What special clues or feelings do you associate with a hit? What clues did you ignore?

Exercise #4: Place Identification

For this exercise, you will need photographs of places and maps that include their sites. The photographs should be of places that are not readily identifiable, but can be pinpointed on a map. The maps can be of a region, country or the world. For example, you might have a photograph of a house in a city.

Ask a friend to assemble photographs of places that are not familiar to you. Look at each photograph, and then dowse their locations on maps. Hold the pendulum over a map and slowly move it over the surface. Follow the actions of the pendulum. When you come close to the location, the pendulum should react with movement. Your psychic sense should indicate the correct location.

How accurate are you? Do you identify the precise location (such as a city) or do you come close (geographic region)?

If you resonate strongly with the pendulum, you are likely to make it your constant companion. I know people who use a pendulum to help them make decisions at work—though they would never admit so to their superiors.

Key #12

The Dream Oracle

The psychic faculty functions in dreams, helping solve problems, obtain guidance, and anticipate events. The importance of dreams as a direct line to higher wisdom has been recognized since ancient times. In these exercises, you will learn how to program your dreams for answers to questions, how to send and receive messages in dreams, and how to use dreams in a precognitive way to look into the future.

Exercise #1: Incubation

People around the world have practiced ways to get answers to specific questions in dreams. These techniques are called dream incubation, from the Greek term *incubatio*, or "sleeping in." We incubate dreams by impressing and holding a request for information within consciousness, so that a desired dream is born into awareness.

The ancients had special places where one went to seek help from the gods through dreams. These were sacred caves, groves, or temples. In the classical world, there were once more than 400 temples devoted to the Greek god of healing, Asklepios. Pilgrims undertook special trips to a temple. Upon arrival, they prepared themselves with rituals of fasting, cleansing, sacrifice and prayer. They went to sleep hoping that Asklepios or one of his helpers, including totem animals, would come to them in their dreams and either heal them or tell them how they could be healed.

You can do dream incubation today right in the sacred temple of your own home. You do not have to remove yourself to the wilderness to tap into this intuitive resource.

Treat dream incubation as a ritual. A ritual is a set of intentions and actions that changes consciousness, thus opening the channels for the Higher Self to speak. The procedure here engages the senses, which heightens the opening of the intuitive channels.

It's a good idea to eat lightly during the day and evening of your incubation. Many old incubation techniques called for fasting, which isn't essential, but a matter of personal preference. Avoid heavy food and alcohol, which can disrupt the sleep cycle.

At the start of the day, frame the question you would like your dreams to answer. Make it simple and clear: "Should I take the new job offer in Chicago?" The simpler your question, the easier it will be to understand your dream's answer. By framing your question early in the day, it will be cooking away in the back of your mind until bedtime. Write the question down in your journal. Think about the question often, followed by an affirmation. For example: "Should I take the new job offer in Chicago? *My dreams will tell me the answer tonight.*"

Prior to bedtime, relax with meditation or inspirational reading. Lighting a candle or burning incense adds to the sensory pleasure of the ritual, thus heightening your anticipation. (But for safety reasons, do not leave an open flame candle burning all night.) Turn your attention to your incubation question. Write it down again. You may want to write it on notepaper and place it beneath your pillow (thus you would literally "sleep on it"). Hold the question and affirmation strongly in your mind. Repeat them silently or out loud three times. Give thanks for the answer that will be revealed.

If you use an alarm, set it a little earlier than usual. You will want to have adequate time to record your dream after you awaken. Recording it is very important, as dreams are quickly forgotten. One method I use to remember dreams is to repeat the dream to myself silently before I get up, which helps to set it into memory. Then I write it down along with my associations and ideas about its meaning. Later, when I have more time, I return to the written account and work with it again.

Record your dream and work with it even if it does not seem to obviously answer your question. The answer may be couched in layers of symbolism.

Sometimes the Dream Oracle responds a night or two later with the answer. And, sometimes the answer doesn't come in dreams, but in waking inspiration and intuition during the day. Your dreaming mind has worked on the question while you sleep, and the answer is presented when it will have the greatest impact upon you. Answers may even come in synchronicities.

When I do dream incubation, I never know how the answer will come, which is what makes this intuitive process so interesting. Sometimes I have a dream that directly addresses the question. Other times I remember little or no dream details, but have the answer clear in my mind as soon as I awaken. Still other times the answer is presented in an event days later.

Don't give up if you feel you're not making progress with the Dream Oracle. You may need to practice a little more. Try rewording the question. Reexamine your dreams to make certain you didn't overlook the answer. If an answer is not the one you're hoping for, it can be passed over.

As you become more adept at dream incubation, experiment with asking increasingly complex questions, such as "If Plan A doesn't work, should I try Plan B?" or "What should I do to accomplish my goal of _____?"

Exercise #2: Sending Messages in Dreams

Dreams are a natural medium for telepathy, the transference of thoughts between or among persons. Scientific experiments and research of dream telepathy have been done over the past century or so. The most famous took place at the Maimonides Medical Center Dream Laboratory in Brooklyn, New York during the 1960s, conducted by Montague Ullman and Stanley Krippner, with psychic Alan Vaughan.

In the experiments, a sender who was awake attempted to telepathically transmit an image, selected at random, to a sleeping recipient in another room. The subject was awakened and asked to describe any dreams. The next day, the subject would view several possible target images and rank them according to how well the images matched the content and emotional tone of their dreams. Overall, the results of these studies were significantly above chance. Researchers noted that team members who had a good rapport achieved better results.

For dream telepathy you will need a partner of any geographic distance. Decide who will be the sender and who will be the recipient. Set a date for dream telepathy: "Next Tuesday night I will transmit something to you." The sender should know the sleep habits of the recipient. There is no point in trying to send a message to dreams at midnight if the recipient is a night owl who stays up until 3 AM. (The recipient may indeed receive the message, but the point here is to use dreams as the medium.) The sender may decide to set the alarm clock for a middle-of-the-night transmission.

Do not give the recipient any clues as to what will be sent. Have several possibilities available, and at the time of transmission, select one at random. Try the following, one at a time:

- A picture of a person or persons
- A picture of an animal
- A picture of a flower or object
- A word
- A short and simple message
- A longer, more complex message

Put several of each on pieces of paper. For images, you can clip photos and drawings from magazines. Keep the papers face down. Use one category at a time.

To transmit, center yourself with Psychic Power Breathing and focus your intent upon connecting to the recipient. Hold a vivid mental image of him or her in your mind; repeat his or her name silently three times. Shuffle your papers and select one. Focus upon the target with as much intensity as possible for fifteen minutes. Make the image or words as vivid as possible.

Meanwhile, the recipient should carefully record dreams upon normal awakening, and later reports the results to the sender. How well did you do? Keep a record.

Go through the complete list in the same roles. Then switch. Try other partners. Compare your results to your relationships. Do you have a higher rate of success with people who share a stronger emotional connection to you?

A variation of this is fun to try whenever you have the opportunity to travel to a time zone significantly different than that of your dream telepathy partner. Set an appointed time for transmission. The sender will focus on an image at random: "At 7 PM my time, which will be 1 AM your time, I will send an image about whatever I will be doing at that moment." The receiver records dream recall upon normal awakening. Later you compare results.

Try the above exercises with groups: one sender, several receivers. When the sender focuses on the image or message to be transmitted, he or she can connect with a group mind or consciousness. There is no need to link to each individual separately.

You can also experiment with unannounced dream telepathy. Make arrangements with a partner or partner that at some unspecified time, you will send them an image or message. Contact them the day after and inquire about their dreams. How well do you get through when you are not expected? Permission in advance to try this is important, out of respect for the privacy of others.

Dream telepathy, like all psychic development exercises, should be treated with consideration. Do not use dream telepathy to send people angry or negative messages. Do not try to program or manipulate others with commands or suggestions. You will not be able to control people or make them do anything they would not ordinarily do.

Dream telepathy is an exciting tool for expansion of consciousness. Stay centered on personal growth, creativity and helping others and your dreaming mind will respond with enthusiasm.

Exercise #3: Dreaming True

You can also ask your dreams to show you the future. According to parapsychological research, extrasensory perception occurs more frequently in dreams than any other medium. An estimated 60 percent of precognition experiences occur in dreams.

Set your intention by asking your dreams to tell you something that will be helpful concerning the future, and that the dreams will be clear in meaning. It is important to ask for helpful information; the Dream Oracle should be used for the highest purpose and not for entertainment. "Dreaming true," or dreaming the future, is distinctly different than ordinary dreaming. Such dreams often have their own peculiar trademark in emotional tone, atmosphere, and signature imagery, and convey a strong certainty upon awakening that the dream will come to pass.

Do not jump to conclusions when trying to dream true. A dream of an earthquake, for example, does not necessarily mean that a real earthquake will happen. An inner earthquake might be pending. Collective fears can influence our dreams, too. In the final years of the twentieth century, the media reported on a seeming increase in doomsday dreaming of natural disasters, wars, and so on. These dreams actually influenced some people to leave their jobs and homes in search of "safe" places. Many of these doomsday dreams actually were reflections of collective fears about "the end times" because of the great turning of the calendar. You must be careful and responsible in interpreting your dreams.

I do believe that more and more, we will see futures in our dreams. We will pierce the veil of time as our intuition skills increase, as our consciousness evolves, and as our spiritual awareness increases. Our ability to look into probable futures will help us make better decisions in the present. We cannot let ourselves be governed by fear; rather, we must allow ourselves to be steered by Truth.

The more you work with your dreams, the more you will appreciate them. Dreams really are your friends. They reflect what is going on within you. They serve the Higher Self, which constantly seeks the best for you.

For more ways to work with pro-active dreaming, see my book *Dreamwork for Visionary Living*.

Key #13

Yes or No

Sometimes the intuitive/psychic sense speaks dramatically, other times subtly. In developing your psychic power, you hone your sensitivity to encourage the subtle signals to speak more emphatically and clearly. You learn your own psychic language, so to speak, and train your ability to add to its vocabulary.

One of the best ways to accomplish this is the Yes or No format. Here are easy exercises that you can do on your own.

Exercise #1: Strengthening Your Psychic Power Vocabulary

You must be thoroughly familiar with how your psychic faculty speaks naturally to you when something is right or wrong. Think of a decision you made, or a course of action that presented itself, that you knew, absolutely knew in every cell of your being, was right for you. What told you it was right? A strong physical sensation? A certain feeling? Visual or auditory clues experienced within, by the inner eye or inner ear? Approval from a guide figure or guardian angel you feel is around you? Re-experience the signals that say "right." Make a list.

Now think of a decision or course of action that was wrong. What signals did you receive in that case? Re-experience, as vividly as possible, how your psychic faculty says "wrong." Make another list.

In both cases, right and wrong, did you follow your signals or override them? What were the consequences of your actions? Think of other cases in which your psychic faculty gave yes-or-no guidance. Did you receive the same kinds of signals?

Are you more likely to pay attention when your psychic sense says "yes" and disregard it when it says "no"? If so, you have plenty of company. It's not unusual to get guidance not to do something, but we proceed to do it anyway, because of all the "oughts" and "shoulds" our rational mind lines up.

Resolve to follow your guidance, even when it runs contrary to the "oughts" and "shoulds." Make a pledge to yourself and your Higher Self in the form of an affirmation:

"I pay attention to my guidance and act in accordance with it."

Repeat this affirmation often on a daily basis.

Review your lists of signals for yes and no. Which are the strongest for each? Focus on those. Identify them with yes or no courses of action. Make more affirmations:

"When I experience _____ I know the answer is yes."
"When I experience _____ I know the answer is no."

For example, you might fill in the blanks with, "When I experience a sensation of expansion and light in my solar plexus, I know the answer is yes," and "When I experience a tightening in my solar plexus, I know the answer is no." You may have more than one signal for yes and no. It's best to work with one or two primary signals at first. You can always expand your vocabulary, as we will see in the next exercise.

Now put your psychic vocabulary into practical application. Every day, make decisions based upon your yes or no signals. Start with small decisions in order to build confidence: travel routes, clothing choices, purchases, food choices, tasks, and so on. Are the skies gray but the weather forecast calls for no rain? Your left brain says that you'd rather not carry around an umbrella if it's not necessary. But what does your intuition tell you? Keep a record of your activities. If you have any misses, analyze how and why you missed the signal. Did you allow any "oughts" or "shoulds" to creep in? Did you allow anyone to dissuade you from a course of action?

Gradually add more important decisions. The more your practice your yes-or-no guidance, the more natural the guidance will become, until you seldom have to stop and think about it. You will be naturally and confidently steered in the right direction.

Exercise #2: Increasing Your Psychic Vocabulary

Practicing intuition exercises has shown you which sense is the dominant medium for you. Everyone is different. You have learn that your psychic sense speaks through images in the inner eye, sounds in the inner ear, feelings and emotions, or physical and tactile sensations.

In this exercise, you will expand your psychic repertoire. Begin with your dominant medium. Choose a pair of opposites to represent yes and no. These will become new signals in your psychic vocabulary.

For example, if visual images are your dominant medium, you might work with:

- red and green traffic lights or flags
- the head and tail of a coin
- thumb up and thumb down
- up arrow and down arrow
- entry sign and exit sign
- smiling face and frowning face
- open door and closed door

You get the idea. If sounds are your dominant medium, pick sounds that are pleasing or harsh to you, or words that are opposite. For example:

- classical music and rap music

- birds singing and jackhammers drilling
- song you like and song you don't like
- the audible words "yes" and "no"
- the audible words "right" and "wrong"
- the audible words "go for it" and "forget it"

Tactile and body sensations might be:

- feeling light and feeling heavy
- tingling and irritation
- expansion and contraction
- relaxation and tension
- energy and fatigue
- hot and cold

Feelings and emotions might be:

- happiness and anxiety
- eagerness and reticence
- joy and sadness

Be creative. Allow whatever arises *psychically* to you to be your new yes-or-no signals. Put some fun into it. The Higher Self has a wonderful sense of humor, and often speaks to us in puns and plays on words. Making it a game invites the inner child to play, and that opens us to territory where the intuition/psychic sense is freer to speak.

How would you use these opposites? When seeking guidance about a choice to make, ask, "Should I do such-and-such? Is this a go-for-it or a forget-it?" Or, "Is it heads up or tails up?" You'll have your answer.

Expand your vocabulary even more by working with signals that are not your dominant medium. If images are your strong suit, try working with sounds. After experimentation, you may decide that you prefer to stick with your dominant medium. But the more you listen to your psychic sense in as many ways as possible, the better receiver you are of all the guidance that comes from the Higher Self.

Key #14

Card Games

Cards are an entertaining way to train your psychic power to see the invisible, sharpen your psychic ability and send your consciousness into archetypal realms.

Cards have served as an important tool in divination throughout history. The most widely used divination methods involve interpretation of random patterns, such as stones, bones or sticks that are cast, or cards that are selected. The random patterns organize information on an intuitive/psychic level.

In the exercises here, you will use cards for psychic "guessing" games, and for archetypal adventures that invite the participation of synchronicity. You can do most of the exercises by yourself; some can be done either alone or with a partner.

Games with Playing Cards

Obtain a deck of regular playing cards and a notepad for tallying your results. Prepare yourself by using Psychic Power Breathing. Spend a few moments stilling your mind.

Exercise #1: Name That Color

This introductory exercise will get you warmed up with card games.

Shuffle the cards and hold them or place them face down. Focus your sensory and psychic attention on the cards until you feel that you "know" them. Focus on the top card. What color is its suit: red or black? Name the color and turn the card over. Were you right? Keep a record of your hits and misses.

You have one-in-two odds of being right by chance. Total your score. Twenty-six is chance. Are you above or below?

Do this exercise two or three times. You will then be ready to move on to the next levels.

Exercise #2: Name That Suit

Shuffle the cards and hold them or place them face down. Focus on the card on top of the deck. What suit is it? Take your time with the answer. When you feel you have it, name the suit and then turn the card over. Go through the entire deck in this manner.

Record each card: the suit you named and the actual suit.

How well did you do? You have a one-in-four chance of guessing the suit correctly. Therefore, out of fifty-two cards, you would expect to get thirteen correct by chance. Total your score of correct answers. Don't be dismayed if you scored less than chance. You probably are trying too hard. Relax and be detached from the outcome. You're not competing for a prize.

Now tally your hits of red versus black. Perhaps you said "diamonds" and the card was a heart. You intuited the color correctly but not the suit. How many of your misses fall into this category?

Repeat this exercise daily and see how your score changes over a period of two weeks. Make notes concerning how you intuit the suits. Do you see mental pictures or have specific body sensations? Does your speed improve? Do you notice better results if you place your palm on top of the card while trying to "see" it?

Exercise #3: Name That Card

Shuffle the deck of cards and hold them face down in your hands. Focus your psychic attention upon them.

Instead of intuiting suits, name the suit and number or court figure: "jack of spades," "seven of hearts," and so on. Take as much time as you need with each card. Remain detached from the outcome. Anxiety and "trying" to be right will inhibit, not help, your performance. Keep a record of your choices and the results.

You will probably find that your score of hits drops considerably when you have to provide more specific information. The more you practice, the more the score will improve. Psychic sense often gives general impressions, but you can hone your skills to significantly improve the amount of detail you perceive.

Do this exercise daily for two weeks and keep track of your results. How much do you improve?

You may notice a curious phenomenon in this and perhaps in exercise #2: you are one or two cards off from being correct. This is called "displacement" in psychical research: we get the correct information, but out of order or out of time sequence. Set your intention to be correct on the mark.

Exercise #4: Cards At Random

Instead of going through the deck in a top-to-bottom sequence, draw out cards at random face down. Identify them and then turn them over. Try drawing cards singly, or drawing several cards at a time.

Exercise #5: Cards by Telepathy

Variations of the above exercises can be done with a partner. The objective is to transmit information about the cards by telepathy. Your psychic faculty is constantly picking up cues from the thoughts and feelings of others. This exercise will help you develop that ability to a higher level of skill.

Decide who will be the sender and who will be the receiver. Sit so that the receiver cannot see the face of the cards. You may sit opposite each other or in different places in the same room. You also can try sitting in separate but adjacent rooms—you must be close enough to hear each other speak.

Both parties should shuffle the deck before each exercise. This forms an energy partnership. Center yourselves with the breath and relaxation.

The sender keeps the deck face down. He picks up the top card from the deck, turns it over and focuses on the image: the color, the suit, or the identity of each card. The recipient should allow the information to arise spontaneously in awareness. When the receiver feels she knows the answer, she writes it down.

The sender keeps the cards in careful order, so that the first card on top of the deck becomes the last card in the stack. The results are then tallied.

Try exercises one through four with a telepathy partner. Change roles. Do the exercises as frequently as possible. Keep track of your improvement. Do you experience displacement with a partner?

Games with ESP Cards

ESP (extrasensory perception) cards are a small deck of symbols that can be used in intuition exercises similar to the ones described above.

ESP cards once were a standard tool in laboratory psychical research for testing ESP, or psi, as it is called now (psi incorporates psychokinesis, the movement of objects with mental power, along with ESP ability). ESP cards still are occasionally used in controlled psi experiments, but for the most part, they have been replaced by the computer. They remain great for personal and in-home use.

The cards were originally named Zener cards after one of their creators. They were first used in 1930 at Duke University in North Carolina, the home of the Institute for Parapsychology and Rhine Research Center. They were created by two Duke faculty members, J.B. Rhine and Karl Zener, as a simplification of psi tests using regular playing cards. Psychical researchers had been using playing cards in tests since the late nineteenth century. The Zener cards were made available for general public use in 1936.

A deck includes twenty-five cards of five symbols each: a star, an equilateral cross, a square, a circle and a set of three wavy horizontal lines, like rippling water. Geometric shapes have proven to be particularly effective in intuition development.

Using ESP cards, you can do all of the exercises described for playing cards. You have a one-in-five chance of being correct.

You can obtain an inexpensive ESP card kit online. Or, you can invent your own symbol cards. Be sure that the card stock is thick enough to prevent any of the images from showing through the backs, and also that all cards are uniform in size.

Games with Tarot Cards

With Tarot cards, the game changes to more of an inner adventure with archetypal images. The Tarot consists of seventy-eight cards and is like two decks in one. A Major Arcana ("Big Mystery") has twenty-two cards bearing images, titles and numbers from zero to twenty-one. A Minor Arcana ("Little Mystery") has fifty-six cards that are similar to modern playing cards: there are four suits, and each suit has four court cards instead of three.

The origin of the Tarot is not known. It may have evolved from playing cards and teaching aids that used images; or, it may have evolved from images used in magical and mystical paths. It came into popular use for games and divination in the eighteenth century. Curious-looking, the cards caught the attention of occultists, who immediately seized upon them as books of secret learning. Most of the theories were more fanciful than factual, such as the cards originated in ancient Egypt, or were spread around Europe by Gypsies who found them in India. Those notions have long since been dispelled. However, the evolution of the cards does show a sophisticated influence of alchemy, magic and the esoteric arts. Today the Tarot is a popular divination and inner work tool.

The language of the Tarot is archetypes: primordial images of unknown origin that have been passed down from an ancestral past that includes not only early humans, but prehuman and animal ancestors. Archetypes are not part of conscious thought, but are predispositions toward certain behaviors—patterns of psychological performance linked to instinct—such as fear of the dark or the maternal instinct, which become filled out and modified through individual experience.

Archetypes are endless, and appear in myth, folk tale and fairy tale. Birth, death, rebirth, power, magic, the sun, the moon, the wind, animals, and the elements are examples of archetypes, as well as are traits embodied in gods and goddesses, the hero, the sage, the judge, the child, the trickster, the earth mother, and other figures such as we find in the Tarot.

Archetypes contain more than can be described by words, which makes them ideal for psychic work. They communicate with the conscious mind in a numinous, or mysterious and transcendent, way. Archetypes speak to us through dreams and through active imagination. When we work with the Tarot, we employ active imagination to engage with images in the archetypal realm. Our intuition/psychic sense loves to roam here. And, this inner work also stimulates dream life.

The real power of the Tarot is not so much in divination, but in the expansion of consciousness into the archetypal realm, which is brimming and alive with spiritual energy, insight and creativity.

Tarot decks proliferate today, designed around themes such as angels and alchemy. The cards are steeped in symbols of an archetypal nature. The Major Arcana is a collection of named and numbered images that portray stages of spiritual enlightenment. The images and their order are fairly consistent from deck to deck, regardless of theme. The Minor Arcana have various names for the four suits, which represent the elements, such as wands (air), staffs (fire), pentacles (earth) and cups (water). Some decks offer pictorial images for all of the Minor Arcana cards, while others use repetitions of the suit signs and thus resemble modern playing cards.

Tarot cards are excellent tools for personal spiritual and intuition work. You do not have to be a Tarot expert to enjoy working with the cards. I have used Tarot cards for many years and find them constantly refreshing and revealing.

For your exercises, you will use the Major Arcana portion of a deck. Select any deck that appeals to you. Many are packaged with companion books that explain the cards. Each of the twenty-two cards in the Major Arcana is an archetypal image that symbolizes a quality, a state of consciousness, a stage of life, a characteristic, or a virtue. Each image has a central figure. For example, The Hierophant is a wise old teacher who symbolizes higher wisdom obtained through learning and study. The Empress, a pregnant queen, represents the ability to bring forth abundance, and to nourish others and ourselves.

The twenty-two cards also form a spiritual journey: our ups and downs as we attempt to move from ignorance to wisdom. We begin our spiritual journey as The Fool (numbered 0), who has not yet been tempered by experience, and end as The World (numbered 21), a state of cosmic consciousness. Along the way, we experience our own magical power to manifest things in the material plane; we learn secrets and mysteries; and we experience unbridled ambition, profound love, material comfort, deprivation, pain, descent into our lower nature, redemption, and rebirth.

These stages of life and states of consciousness provide rich material for the psychic faculty. By working with archetypal images, we invite the Higher Self to offer commentary on what we are doing in life.

The following is a list of the Major Arcana cards and their best-known names:

    0 The Fool
    1 The Magician
    2 The High Priestess
    3 The Empress
    4 The Emperor
    5 The Hierophant
    6 The Lovers
    7 The Charioteer
    8 Justice
    9 The Hermit
    10 The Wheel of Fortune
    11 Strength
    12 The Hanged Man
    13 Death
    14 Temperance
    15 The Devil
    16 The Tower
    17 The Star
    18 The Moon
    19 The Sun
    20 Judgment
    21 The World

Examine the cards closely. You will see that each card is a storyteller, and the story invites you to go deeper into the images. Take some time to familiarize yourself with them.

Exercise #1: Mirror, Mirror

Take the Major Arcana and get comfortable for meditation. Use Psychic Power Breathing and relaxation to center yourself and quiet the mind. Turn over the top card on your stack.

Contemplate the image. Notice every detail. What does the card have to say to you? What is its story?

Imagine a gateway before you and allow yourself to become one with the card. What does the image have to say about you and to you? For example, how do you embody Justice? Perhaps it is a weak area for you rather than a strength. Does Justice have a "pay attention" message for you?

Allow your psychic power to speak to you through the card. Ask for whatever is needed for you at this time. Thoughts and images will arise. Absorb them, but do not try to control or direct them. Make notes in your journal.

The mysteries in each card are vast, and in any one session, you will see only a small part of the whole. Perhaps you will be shown something related to a lesson you must learn in this life. Or, you will be given the answers to questions you have long sought. Perhaps you will be escorted to the cosmic Hall of Wisdom.

No two meditative excursions through the Major Arcana are the same, even with the same card.

Work with the cards one by one in order. Contemplate and meditate on one each day. After you've gone through the deck, continue to work with the cards when you feel drawn to them. Pull a card at random or select one that calls to you.

Exercise #2: Archetype for a Day

Center with Psychic Power Breathing and relaxation. Shuffle the Major Arcana. Set your intention with this affirmation, *"I will select the archetype I need to work with today."*

Draw a card at random. As you did in the previous Mirror, Mirror exercise, contemplate the card and take notes of what it has to tell you.

As you go throughout your day, pay attention to how you encounter this archetype through synchronicity. Let's say that you draw Justice again. Perhaps you will see pictures, videos, or film of court scenes or depictions of justice or injustice. Perhaps you will engage in an argument and seek a solution of fairness. Perhaps you will be confronted with someone's revenge as a way of justice. Perhaps you will know psychically how to end a dispute.

At the end of the day, record your experiences in your journal. How did you live the Archetype for a Day? What insights and lessons did you learn?

Exercise #3: Dreaming the Tarot

This exercise invites your psychic power to work with both Tarot and dream images.

Before bedtime, shuffle the Major Arcana and select a card at random. Contemplate the card and what it has to say to you.

Affirm three times, *"My psychic power will use (name of card) to give me a message in my dreams tonight."*

When you awaken, record your dream and interpret it through dreamwork. The image of the card may not be present in your dream. Focus on the message of the dream and how it relates to the card.

You are likely to invent your own exercises with playing cards, ESP cards, and the Tarot. Keep a notebook.

Key #15

The Open Book

The Open Book is a good skill-sharpening exercise that you can do on your own.

You will need the white pages of any telephone book. Sit comfortably with the phone book on your lap or in front of you. Do Psychic Power Breathing to center your consciousness and stimulate the third eye.

Close your eyes and open the phone book to any page. Run your finger down the page and stop wherever you wish. Using your inner vision, try to "see" the name your finger is pointing to. The response that arises spontaneously *first* in your mind is the answer. Do not try to "think" about it or make a rational guess ("Let's see, I should be in the M's, so maybe it is Madison..."). You want your psychic mind, not your logical, deductive reasoning mind, to do the "thinking."

Open your eyes and compare your answer to the name your finger has selected.

You may find that you were wildly off the mark. Or you may be surprised at just how accurate you were.

Do the Open Book exercise for fifteen to twenty minutes several times a week. It's important to do it for a stretch of time–not just a minute or two–in order to get a psychic flow of energy going. Vary the exercise by picking out phone numbers or addresses (such as the name of a street) instead of people names. Be adventurous and try for all three at once.

You may find yourself "seeing" the name just above or below the name your finger selects. This displacement is not uncommon in psychic work. The Open Book exercise will help you hone your accuracy.

Keep a record of your hits and misses, and observations you have around them. For example, your misses may occur when you allow guesses and deductive reasoning to sneak into the process. The record will show you how quickly you progress, and will increase your awareness of how your psychic sense speaks to you. Make note of emotions and physical sensations. Did you feel an electrical tingle whenever you "knew" you were right? Or a tightening sensation when you were wrong?

Do not be alarmed if you experience a period of many misses. The psychic faculty goes through cycles of peaks and valleys, just as do our emotions, mental clarity and physical energy.

Variations

You can try other books besides the telephone book for this exercise. The dictionary is a good alternative. Large scriptural works, such as the Bible, Torah, or Quran, are good. Avoid books that you read often, as you will be too familiar with their contents. Your memory of what material lies where in the book will interfere with the psychic faculty.

Key #16

Future News

Now it's time to exercise your ability to see into the future. The Future News exercise is based on a test once used in psychical research with mediums.

In the so-called "newspaper tests," done under controlled circumstances, a medium would give information from the next day's newspaper before the newspaper went to press. Information included names of people featured in stories, page numbers, and positions of stories, headlines, news events and so on. The information supposedly came from the medium's spirit helper, called a "control." The purpose of the newspaper test was to provide evidence in support of survival after death by showing that the information given at the sittings was beyond the subconscious knowledge possessed by either the medium or observers. In other words, it had to come from the realm of discarnate spirits.

These tests were especially popular after World War I, when many grieving families sought to communicate with victims of the war through mediums. Psychical researchers in turn sought to test the ability of mediums to try to find proof of survival.

The idea for newspaper tests came from Gladys Osborne Leonard, a famous British medium who had excelled at "book tests," or giving accurate information from books in distant locations. Leonard worked with a control named "Feda." Leonard was very good at her book and newspaper tests. The newspaper tests were especially significant because they were conducted before press time, and thus psychical researchers felt they could rule out clairvoyance. However, they did not consider that clairvoyance operates outside of linear time, and we can use this ability to see into the past and the future.

We have a much different and better understanding of psi today. Spirit guides and survival after death may have been the focus in those earlier times, but today we look upon such tests as evidence in support of precognition and clairvoyance/remote viewing, something we can accomplish by projecting our consciousness.

In the Future News exercise, you will use your psychic ability to read the news events that are yet to happen. Many people read or listen to the news on the internet now instead of reading hard print newspapers. This exercise can be adapted to whatever format you use.

Relax in a comfortable seated position, and do Psychic Power Breathing as preparation for the exercise. Close your eyes and visualize before you the news of tomorrow. Make the visualization as vivid as possible. If you are reading a hard print newspaper, mentally hold it and feel the texture and weight of it in your hands. Smell the newsprint and ink. See tomorrow's date clearly printed on the banner. Now read the major headline on the front page. What will tomorrow's news be?

If you are reading news on a computer or cellphone screen, follow the same procedure. Feel your device in your hands, and call up a digital news report for the next day on the screen.

Take a deep breath and let the news image dissolve. Open your eyes and record your experience in your intuition journal. Make note of any physical or emotional sensations that are part of the experience.

On the morrow, check the news against what you saw with your inner eye. Get a copy of the newspaper or access the online news page. How accurate was your vision of the headline? Did you see some of the same words, perhaps key words? Did you see a similar, but not same, event? Perhaps you saw news of an accident, but the kind of accident was wrong.

Do this exercise every day. The best time is in the morning, before you have been exposed to any news that might subconsciously influence you (such as the latest developments in an ongoing news story). Do not try to anticipate news based on knowledge you already have. As we know from experience, any day can bring surprises in the news.

Make the Future News exercise more complex as you progress:

- Increase the number of headlines you see. Note their position on the page or screen. Open the newspaper or scroll down and read different pages. Note the headlines and the numbers of the pages they are on.
- Read the stories under the headlines to learn details.
- Advance in time. See the news that will be published in a week's time. Pick a date several months away and read that news with the inner eye. Does your accuracy change the farther out you move in time? Perhaps you allowed doubt about your ability to see the far future to affect your accuracy.

Reading the Future News has been done successfully by many people looking for advantages for financial investment. For example, they seek to see stock quote prices on a given day.

The Future News also can help you plan your travel and make other decisions affected by news events.

Key #17

Hide and Seek

How often have you had a sudden and unexpected thought about someone, only to find out later that they were thinking of you at about the same time? This sort of experience happens frequently, and is a splendid example of your psychic power at work. You and the other person spontaneously used your psychic sense to tune in to each other. Perhaps your thoughts were colored by emotions or gave you a sense of what the other person might be doing. Perhaps you let the thoughts pass pleasantly, or perhaps you felt inspired to action, such as calling the other person.

This psychic contact with another person can be deliberate as well as spontaneous. As we saw in the previous exercise, we can, through remote viewing (see Key #8), tune in to distant places and people.

Exercise #1: Basic Hide and Seek

Hide and Seek is a fun exercise that blends a childhood game with remote viewing. You will need a partner. You can play this with a friend, family member or spouse.

Select a day as Target Day. You must spend this day apart. One of you will be the viewer and the other the target. If you know your partner well, select a day that will *not* be one of routine activities that you can anticipate in advance. Ideally, you should not know where the target person will be and what he or she will be doing.

At three agreed-upon check-in times, the viewer will use psychic power to see where the target is and what the target is doing. The target must jot down a few notes about his or her location and activities at the appointed times. Have no other contact throughout the day.

At the end of the day, compare notes. How accurate was the viewer? Were specific surroundings intuited? Colors? Emotional tones? Perhaps impressions were general rather than specific. For example, you might have received an impression of traveling while your target was on a bus, but no details about the bus or where it was going.

Did the target experience any unusual thoughts or intuitions at the same time? Was there a reciprocal remote viewing?

Try the exercise again on another day and switch roles. Vary Hide and Seek with other partners, including people whom you do not know well.

Here's how Hide and Seek worked for Jo, who used her psychic remote viewing to tune in to a woman she knew casually. She did not know exactly where she, the "beacon," was located. Note how Jo allowed her rational thought to interfere with and assess her intuitive impression:

> On tuning in to her, I rapidly had a very strong impression of whiteness, which then settled to a white house quite distinctive in shape with eight or nine windows. There were some windows in the roof and an attractively shaped section where the roof met the vertical wall of the house. It was curved in the Dutch style. In the center of the main curve was an ornately outlined oval medallion shape.
>
> Logic then started to invade. I kept thinking that the reason I was seeing something with a Dutch influence was because the beacon [target] was Dutch herself. But my first impression was correct. The house did have a strong Dutch style to it. I remember having an odd feeling in the solar plexus as the first impression came in.

Jo's first impression, which came rapidly, was of a Dutch-style house. This was accurate. Yet she allowed her knowledge of the target, a Dutch woman, to interfere with the impression.

It cannot be over-emphasized that the impressions that arise spontaneously and quickly are accurate. When we try to interpret or analyze them prematurely, we risk distorting them. Note that Jo received a visceral, physical confirmation of her first impression with an "odd" feeling in the solar plexus. Do not ignore your signals. You do not known what you are "supposed" to perceive.

Exercise #2: Future Hide and Seek

Now you are going to stretch your psychic sense to look into the future. Select another Target Day with your partner, but do not discuss appointed check-in times or any planned activities. At the start of the day, spend some quiet time in meditation, and center with Psychic Power Breathing. Select a time later in the day and ask your psychic sense where your partner will be and what he or she will be doing. Write down your impressions.

Check with your partner at the end of the day to see how your advance impressions matched the events that took place. Do this exercise often, and switch roles and work with different partners.

Try looking farther into the future. Pick a day a week away or a month away, and a specific time. Record your impressions. On the Target Day, remind your partner to pay attention to places, activities and times. Then compare notes at the end of the day.

When looking into someone else's activities, it is important to do so *only* with their knowledge and permission. Developing the psychic faculty is for personal growth and betterment, and spiritual development as well, and is not for personal spy games.

Hide and Seek can help to foster a strong psychic bond between people. The ability to tune into another person's safety and whereabouts can bring peace of mind when other means of communication are not possible.

How to tune in

The Hide and Seek exercise will reveal to you the ways to tune in that work best for you. Experiment with these techniques:

- Visualize as vividly as possible the other person's face. Keep your attention to the face. You may not know what he or she is wearing. Allow those details to be filled in by the intuition.

- Mentally repeat the person's name. See the name written on your inner screen.
- Hold an object belonging to the person while doing one or both of the above. Or, look at a photograph of the person. The addition of psychometry can be helpful.
- Hold a mental picture of the two of you linking hands.
- Imagine a searchlight emanating from your third eye which travels across time and space and illuminates what you wish to see and know.

Key #18

Messages in Voices

A person's voice conveys far more information that the words it expresses. We use our voice in many ways as part of our body language. The tone of our voice can add emphasis to our words or it can belie them. We respond instinctively to the sound and quality of voices. We respect and are swayed strong, confident voices; we disregard weak and timorous voices. Often we are affected less by the actual words spoken and more by the sound of the voice.

As a writer, I interview many people of all walks in life for many purposes: fact gathering, expert opinions, confidential perspectives, personal information, and more. I often interview people about intensely personal and sensitive experiences. In almost all cases, I am a stranger to them, yet I am asking them to trust me in giving me the information that I seek. On numerous occasions, people have commented voluntarily to me that there was "something" in my voice that made them feel completely comfortable and at home with me.

The voice is an important key to psychic power. The undercurrents of sound contain information transmitted as mental and emotional impressions. The psychic person learns to listen holistically, that is, to all the dimensions of the spoken word: the words themselves, and the information carried by the vibration of sound. In the cases described above, the interviewees' natural psychic sense tuned into my voice and gave them impressions, perhaps telling them of my sincerity, interest, professionalism, or whatever that instilled in them a feeling of comfort and trust.

Exercise #1: Voice Attunement

This exercise can be done in pairs or in small groups. If done in small groups, keep the number to six or less in order to keep the flow of energy at a good pace. Prepare by relaxing, centering and the doing Psychic Power Breathing. While the others listen, one person speaks in a normal conversational tone. The person should begin by stating his or her name, followed by anything that comes to mind. For example, "My name is Edmund Smith, and I live in Rochester, New York. I work as a computer programmer, and I like to ski and play golf." Or, "My name is Alicia Benton. Last Saturday I went to the Museum of Fine Arts and saw an exhibit of impressionist paintings. After that I had coffee... etc."

It's important to state one's name, for we subtly convey much about ourselves in the ways we say our names. The rest of the little monologue provides time for the listeners to tune in to the voice. The speaker should talk for about a minute or so. Listeners may want to close their eyes in order to focus attention.

When the person is done speaking, the listeners then take turns giving their tactful psychic impressions that arose during the exercise. They may be impressions directly about the person, or they may seem to have little, if anything, to do with him or her. These should be offered, anyway, as they are likely to have a personal meaning to the speaker, perhaps relating to something they're thinking about, or a situation they're dealing with. For example: "While you were talking, I kept seeing an ocean liner..." You may find out the speaker has business dealings with cruise ships, or is preparing to take a cruise vacation.

After everyone has offered their impressions, the listener provides feedback on the "hits." The listener should refrain from offering feedback, even in the form of expressions or nods of the head, until all have spoken. Otherwise, reactions might influence other participants to modify their reports of the impressions they received. Listeners should avoid labeling any impressions as "wrong." Rather, choose language such as "I don't feel that fits," or "I can't relate much to that." Sometimes we don't see the connections right way.

Go around the circle until everyone has had an opportunity to be the speaker.

Experiment with closing your eyes and keeping them open during listening. Closing them may help you a great deal, especially in the beginning, but you should increase your practice with them open. The reason is simple and practical. In everyday life, we converse with people with our eyes open. Trying to talk to someone whose eyes are closed is disconcerting. Furthermore, the psychic faculty also benefits from the visual impressions that are received.

After you've practiced with listening to short speeches, try a variation. The speaker simply gives his or her full name. That's it. You may think that just a name isn't enough to generate much in the way of impressions, but don't let yourself be limited. You'll probably surprise yourself with the amount of impressions you receive.

The truth of the matter is, you have been receiving psychic voice impressions all along whenever you have interacted with others. Unless these impressions were strong, they went unnoticed on a conscious level, but were absorbed on a subconscious level. Now you have expanded your awareness to take more notice of them.

Exercise #2: Voices on the Telephone

Now try your voice attunement on the telephone. Listen to people with your psychic sense as well as your ears. What impressions do you receive? Jot them down while you are talking. If you have the opportunity, validate your impressions by asking questions.

In addition, you can exercise your psychic faculty with these telephone games:

- When the telephone rings, identify the caller before you answer or look at caller ID.
- Or, identify the caller *and* the purpose of the call before you answer.

- When you make a call, determine how many rings will sound before the call is answered.
- Determine whether the call will be answered by a person or voice mail.
- If any of various persons could answer the telephone, identify who will answer in advance.

What benefit are voice impressions? They are especially useful when you meet someone for the first time, or when you are called upon to make decisions based upon what you are being told. Can you trust someone? Have they done their homework? Impressions also will help you to find the right words to say to another, especially in sensitive situations.

Key #19

Colored Dots

In Tibetan dream yoga, visualizations involving colored balls of light are used, along with mantra and body positions, to facilitate lucid dreaming as a path to enlightenment. The dream yoga opens the inner eye. The two exercises here are similar to dream yoga, in that they employ colored dots or balls of light to focus attention inward. The inward focus encourages the psychic faculty to expand.

Exercise #1: Orange Dot
    For the Orange Dot exercise, you will need a piece of orange paper and one or more 25-watt blue light bulbs. The blue light bulbs are not expensive, and you can find them in most grocery or variety stores.
    Take the orange paper and cut out a circle about three to four inches in diameter. The easiest way to do this is to trace around the bottom of a drinking glass.
    Select a room in your home where you will do this exercise. You will need to sit comfortably (not lie down) and look up at a wall. The objects and furnishings in the room will not matter, for your attention will be directed to the orange dot.

Tape the orange dot high up on a wall, but not so high that you have to crane your neck to see it from a chair or sofa. Arrange seating so that you face the dot.

Place one or two blue light bulbs in the lamps in the room. The number of bulbs you need will depend on the size of the room. You will use only blue light to illuminate the room. The blue light will make it difficult to see objects in the room clearly, and the eyes will get tired quickly. Thus, external distractions will recede from attention and the inner eye will take over. The room will be dimly lit, but you should have enough blue light to see the orange dot on the wall.

With the blue light suffusing the room, settle comfortably into your chair or sofa. Relax and do some Psychic Power Breathing to circulate the universal life force and open the third eye.

Focus your attention on the orange dot. Try to bring the orange dot off the wall and make it travel to your third eye. Spend twenty to thirty minutes on this exercise. If you lose concentration or can make the orange dot travel only part way, start again.

It is helpful to play some soft mediation music in the background. I use this exercise with a tape that plays about twenty minutes on a side. I do the exercise until one side is finished. The music helps me maintain concentration, and also not think about how much time is passing.

Initially, nothing may happen with the orange dot. Do not be concerned, but keep practicing. You will find that the orange dot will seem to expand or change shape, and will seem to come off the wall and travel in space. If you cannot bring it to your third eye, it does not mean you have failed the exercise. The act of focusing on the orange dot and attempting to bring it to your third eye is the essence of it. The inner eye will open. You may find psychic flashes occurring to you while you do this exercise.

Do the Orange Dot exercise three or four times a week. I find that evening near bedtime is ideal. The exercise itself is very relaxing, and it also facilitates productive dreaming. Avoid the television, radio, internet, or busy work after you're done.

If you don't have a blue light bulb handy, you can still do this exercise effectively in regular but dim light. Blue light works a little more quickly.

Exercise #2: Red Dot

The Red Dot exercise is simple yet very effective. It requires nothing more than your imagination, and can be done anywhere anytime.

Relax with Psychic Power Breathing. Close your eyes and imagine that a clean white screen covers your entire field of inner vision.

Now place a red dot or ball of light at the far left side of the screen. Slowly move the red dot in an arc across the screen to the right side. Then move the dot in an arc back to the left side, and so on, back and forth. Continue for as long as you can maintain concentration. If thoughts intrude, let them dissolve. Start over by establishing the clear white screen and red dot at the far left.

As in the Orange Dot exercise, moving the red dot will strengthen your inner vision. This is a great "inner eye workout" that you can do in moments of idle time. Try starting the day with it.

Key #20

Shapes and Symbols

The visualization of geometric shapes strengthens psychic power by exercising the right brain and training the mind to concentrate. A trained mind organizes information more efficiently, and organized information is simplified information.

Do these exercises during meditation. Like other exercises in this book, you can also do them during "down time" such as waiting in a line or riding as a passenger in a vehicle.

Center yourself with Psychic Power Breathing and relaxation. Close your eyes.

Imagine a black screen before you at eye level, like a blackboard at school. You are going to visualize a series of geometric shapes in white upon the screen. Hold each image steady for about three minutes, then move on to the next one.

Start with a circle. Place it in the center of your black screen. Hold the image still. If distracting thoughts arise, gently release them, like water flowing through a sieve. You may find that the image wants to change by altering its shape or color, or moving around on the black screen. Whenever it shifts, gently return it to its original form. After you have held the white circle for several minutes, allow it to dissolve on the screen. Bring up another shape in white. Follow the same procedure.

Here are more shapes to work with:

- Circle with a dot in the center
- Square
- Square with a dot in the center
- Equilateral triangle
- Equilateral triangle with a dot in the center
- Equilateral triangle with a circle inside it
- Circle with an equilateral triangle inside it
- Circle with a square inside it
- Equilateral cross
- Square with equilateral cross inside it
- Five-pointed star
- Six-pointed star
- Cube

You can add your own shapes, such as symbols that are meaningful to you. For example, I often use a rose, which is the symbol of perfection. Stick to simple symbols that can be easily sketched in white upon your black screen.

Do as many shapes and symbols as you can in a session without becoming mentally fatigued.

Key #21

Mirror Images

Using your psychic power means being able to see, or perceive, the unseen. You "know" and "see" what is not obvious to the physical senses and ordinary thought processes. In order for the inner eye to see better, you retrain the physical eyes to look beyond the physical.

One of the best and most often-used tools for inner eye training since ancient times is the mirror, or any shiny, flat, and reflective surface.

Gazing upon shiny surfaces is one of the oldest forms of *scrying*, an ancient method of divination. Throughout history, scrying has been used to look into the future, answer questions, solve problems, find lost objects and people, and identify or find criminals.

"Scrying" comes from a Middle English word *descry*, which means "to succeed in discerning" or "to make out dimly." The tool of scryers, called a speculum, can be any object that works for an individual, but usually is one with a reflective surface. The oldest and most common speculum is still water in a lake, pond or dark bowl. Ink, blood and other dark liquids have been used for centuries. Nostradamus scryed with a dark bowl of water or ink set upon a brass tripod. He dipped a wand into the water and anointed himself with a few drops, then gazed into the bowl until he saw visions.

Other specula include glass fishing floats, polished metals and stones, crystal balls and precious gems. John Dee, the royal magician to Queen Elizabeth I, used a crystal egg and a black obsidian mirror. In Arab countries, scryers use their own polished thumbnails. Black mirrors are increasingly popular today, and I teach many black mirror gazing workshops for contacting the dead and spirits, seeing into the past and future, and visiting the astral plane.

Inner eye exercises with mirrors are easy and can be done on your own. Do the following exercises in dim light. Remember from the Colored Dots exercises that dim light tires the physical eyes and thus enables the inner eye to take over. If you turn lights completely off and sit in the dark, you are more likely to get sleepy and doze off. Dim light will keep you mentally alert.

Do not try to anticipate or force results. Do not worry if nothing seems to happen at the time. You may get your psychic flashes afterwards.

Exercise #1: Faces in the Mirror
In a dimly lit room, sit in front of a mirror. Center and relax with Psychic Power Breathing. As your eyes adjust to the light, regard yourself in the mirror. Focus on your face. Observe as much detail as possible—the contour and shape of your features, the angles of the face, the way your hair falls on the skin, and so on. Be detached, not judgmental. This is not an assessment of what you like or don't like, but a neutral observation of what is. In the dim light, your features will not be sharp and clear. Just observe.

Then pull back your perspective from detail to the whole. Look at your whole face. Hold the gaze as long as possible. When the image begins to blur, allow it to do so. If your thoughts wander, refocus on your face. Become aware of your breath. Continue the focus.

At some point, your awareness will shift. It may be sudden and marked, or it may be subtle and steal upon you. Your face may begin to change in the mirror, altering in shape or features. In fact, you may look completely different. Some people feel that the mirror reveals the faces of past lives.

You may see other visions in the mirror, such as scenes, people, and objects. You are likely to see these better with your averted or peripheral vision. Information, or an awareness, may come along with these visions. Take mental notes.

You may see nothing in the mirror except yourself, but instead have a flood of psychic thoughts, inspirations, ideas, and knowledge. You may hear things distinctly with the inner voice, which may sound audible.

You will know when you are ready to stop the exercise. You will feel "full" or you will be tired. Recenter yourself with Psychic Power Breathing. Then record your experience in your journal.

Exercise #2: Third Eye Gazing

Sit comfortably in front of a small mirror. You can position a little mirror on a table top or dresser, or hang a small mirror on a wall at eye level. Dim the lights in the room. Relax and center with Psychic Power Breathing.

Look into the mirror and focus your attention on the third eye, the spot in the forehead that is in the center of, and slightly above, the brows. Imagine a diamond of light there. Become aware of the breath, and feel the breath pulsing as energy through the third eye. Let thoughts dissolve.

Maintain the focus for as long as you can. The diamond of light may change shape or grow in size. Be aware of other imagery that may appear around you, or intuitive thoughts or words.

When you are ready to stop, recenter yourself. Record your experience.

Exercise #3: Scrying for Answers

Now that you have practiced seeing with the inner eye in mirrors, try your expanding psychic ability on specifics, such as making decisions and seeing into the future. Formulate a single question to ask. It is best to stick to a single question, especially in the beginning, in order to get the clearest response. Examples are "Will I..." "Should I..." "Will Plan A be a success?" and so on. You can also ask questions about timing: "When should I..."

Choose either Exercise #1 or Exercise #2. After you have settled in front of the mirror and relaxed, ask your question. Then focus your attention on the mirror. Keep the question foremost in your mind. Repeat it several times silently.

What response do you get? Images, thoughts, sounds, feelings? When you have the answer, you will know with a distinct signal in the manner that your psychic sense speaks to you, such as an *aha!* feeling, a tingling of the skin, or a warm feeling in the abdomen.

If you receive no answer while gazing into the mirror, remain confident that it will come at the appropriate moment.

Record your experience.

Exercise #4: Mirror of the Future

You can ask the mirror to show you the future.

Follow the steps for Exercise #1 or Exercise #2. As you gaze into the mirror, state out loud your request. If you wish to see your future, say, "Reveal my future." The request can be made specific, such as, "Reveal my future concerning _____."

The mirror may respond with visual images, or you may receive a "knowing" within. Record your experience. Note any dates or time periods that you can check against the accuracy of what you are given.

Black Mirror Variations

The above exercises can also be done with a black mirror instead of a silver one. Black mirrors are glass painted or coated black on the reverse side. Many people, myself included, prefer black mirrors because they offer a blank surface, like a blackboard, that allows images to arise more easily.

Black mirrors should also be used in dimly lit rooms. In Exercises #3 and #4, position the mirror so that you do not see yourself in it. Also minimize the reflections of objects around you. Sometimes laying the mirror flat so that it points up at the ceiling works the best. You can still gaze into the mirror at an angle.

For more information on black mirrors and their psychic uses, see my book *The Art of Black Mirror Scrying*.

Key #22

Lotus Eye

The sixth chakra, which sits between and slight above the brows, is instrumental in your psychic and spiritual vision. The more you devote yourself to developing your psychic power, the more you increase your understanding of the spiritual side of life. The sixth chakra becomes stimulated, and expands your vision, self-knowledge, and connection to the Source.

The sixth chakra is called the third eye, because it sees the unseen. It is a lamp that illuminates the darkness of uncertainty. It is also called the lotus eye. In Eastern philosophy, the lotus represents beauty, sanctity, and the true nature of all beings. The chakras themselves are often portrayed as lotus flowers with many petals. Think of the sixth chakra as a lotus flower opening to full bloom as you progress in your psychic development.

You will need a partner for the Lotus Eye exercise.

Sit facing each other, close together, in a room with dim or blue light. If you have candles, place a lit one between you. If you wish, play soft, meditative music in the background. Relax and center with Psychic Power Breathing. One of you will be the sender and one the receiver.

Both of you know at the outset of the exercise that you will attempt to establish a link through your lotus eyes, and the sender will give a message to the receiver.

Set a timer for ten minutes.

Both of you bring your attention to the third eye of your partner. See it as a brilliant white lotus blossom unfolding its petals.

The person who is the receiver remains focused and passive.

The sender bathes the receiver in an energy of unconditional love. Appreciate the soul beauty of that person, wishing for him or her the highest possible good, the achievement of dreams, and the enjoyment of love, prosperity, health, and happiness.

Then acknowledge the connection between the two of you, staying focused on the lotus eye. Psychic impressions about the person may arise. Allow them to unfold. Make mental notes.

Keeping your attention on the lotus eye, and keeping love and acceptance in your consciousness, send the partner a mental message. Direct it to their lotus eye. Keep it short, such as a word, phrase, sound, or simple picture. Do not try to preconceive a message before you start. Allow the message to arise spontaneously. Be absolutely sincere. Put as much energy as you can into it.

When the timer sounds, both of you recenter with Psychic Power Breathing. Compare experiences. The receiver speaks first, describing feelings, thoughts, images, tactile sensations, and impression of a message. Don't guess or try to fill in where nothing was experienced. If there was no distinct impression of a message, say so.

The sender then describes his or her experience and psychic impressions, and states the message. The receiver may discover that the message was cloaked in symbols, feelings or other imagery.

Now switch roles and do the exercise again, setting the timer for ten minutes.

In the beginning, most people have a small amount of difficulty in understanding the message. Do this exercise frequently, with different partners, to increase your skill. What you are learning is telepathy and the sharing of thoughts, which is a function of the third eye. You are learning how to "read" people without speaking.

The purpose of this exercise is not to invade the thoughts of others, but to accurately sense what they are thinking or feeling, so that you can make the best possible response. People often say one thing when they really mean another. Or, they don't say what they really want. The best negotiators and the best sales people have keen psychic sense. They see the big picture. Their lotus eye gives clues as to what to say or do to encourage others to respond favorably. They know when to keep pressing and when to quit.

The Lotus Eye exercise also helps you to convey your message—your conviction, feelings, persuasion, ability, and sincerity—to others in powerful, unspoken ways. Sometimes people are not swayed so much by words as by a "feeling" they have about you. This is your char charisma. Like the blossom of the lotus, it's waiting to unfold in you.

Part III
Using Your Psychic Power

7

Practical Psychic Power

Now that you have practiced the exercises in the twenty-two Keys, you have become familiar with your psychic power and how it works you. You should be reaping the benefits of it daily. You can ask your psychic sense to help you on demand, anytime you need to make a decision, or whenever you face choices about something important. You can also ask it to help you improve your relationships and finances, expand your creativity, and further your self-improvement. Your psychic ability can assist you in healing. And, it can help you break through to a new level of visionary thinking.

An activation plan

Follow these steps to activate your power for all of your goals:

1. Set a clear objective. Situations can be a tangle of short-term, long-term, and even conflicting needs. You must be clear about your central purpose. "My objective is to be the top-ranking sales person in the company." "My objective is to improve my marriage." "My objective is to inspire people with my work."

2. Ask a clear question. You will get the best results with questions that can be answered with a yes or no. "Should I take over the XYZ account?" "Should I take the job offer?" "Should I ask my spouse to see a counselor with me?" However, as you gain more experience you can pose questions that are more complex, for example, "Tell me the best way to..." or "How can I..." or "Tell me the best way to achieve my objectives."

3. Gather data. Psychic ability does not operate in a vacuum. It helps you see more clearly that which you already know and understand. Information is your best friend. Do your research and your homework thoroughly.

4. Ask for guidance. Seek out the opinions of others. Ask for inner guidance.

5. Evaluate what you have gathered. Your rational mind will leap to the chance to sift and sort. Allow the psychic faculty to play a strong hand. Sometimes the facts and figures look good, but don't "feel" right.

6. Take action. Follow through. You'll benefit from the process only if you act on it.

In this section, you will find a collection of exercises and guided meditations to help you in all areas of life. Use them, and let them inspire you to develop more exercises of your own.

8

Getting The Message

Here are exercises that will stimulate psychic breakthroughs. Use them for any situation. Set your objective and question. Prepare for each exercise with Psychic Power Breathing and relaxation found in Keys #1 and #2.

Exercise #1: Calling the Inner Guide

Close your eyes and let yourself travel to a beautiful garden. The sun is shining, the air is warm, and all around you flowers are in full bloom. Relax and appreciate the peace and beauty. Let all of your senses drink in your surroundings. You are on a path that meanders through the garden. Walking along, you see a bench ahead of you on the side of the path. Sit down on the bench.

You notice a presence approaching you along the path. It may be a person. It may be an animal. It may be someone or something mysterious—perhaps an angel or a spirit guide. This is the inner guide you have chosen to represent the wisdom of your Higher Self.

Greet your guide with a welcome and thanks. Ask for its name.

Your guide has a message for you. It is precisely what you need to know, the answer to your question. Receive the answer and thank your guide for helping you.

Return now along the garden path. Recenter yourself and when you're ready open your eyes. Write down additional thoughts.

Once you have made contact with the Inner Guide, you can summon its help anytime by calling to mind an image of it, and/or calling its name. In mystical and magical traditions, names provide access to power.

You can have many Inner Guides. You may work with a group of them, or a succession of them. They may appear in dreams, waking visions, and in synchronistic experiences.

Exercise #3: Email from Your Higher Self

Close your eyes and imagine yourself at your desk at home or at work. Sit down at your computer and go online. You are informed that you have email waiting. Open your mail. You have one email, and it is from your Higher Self.

The email answers your question. It may be with a single word. Or, your Higher Self may have written you a longer letter full of advice and insight.

Read the email and save it in a special file. Send a reply note giving thanks.

Recenter yourself and when you feel ready open your eyes. Write down any additional thoughts.

As in the exercise above, you can carry on an email conversation with your Higher Self.

Exercise #4: Phone Call from God

Close your eyes and imagine yourself comfortable at home. The telephone rings. You answer. God is calling you with the answer to your question.

When the message is delivered or the conversation is completed, give thanks and hang up. Recenter yourself and when you feel ready open your eyes. Write down any additional thoughts.

Exercise #5: Message in a Bottle

Close your eyes and imagine yourself at the seashore. You are alone, walking along the beach at water's edge. You feel relaxed and at peace, enjoying the crunch of the sand and the cool water lapping at your feet. The air is full of salt.

Looking down, you notice something shiny just ahead of you. You pick it up. It is a bottle, brought in by the tide. It is sealed and has a piece of paper inside.

You open the bottle and pull out the paper. It has a message written on it. The message is addressed to you and answers your question. You are elated. The universe has sent you a letter. Looking down again, you see a whole sand dollar. It is your lucky sign that this message is indeed right for you.

Exercise #6: Out of the Woods

Sometimes situations are so complicated that it is difficult to get a handle on them. You think that if only you could see things more clearly you would know what to do. This exercise will help you "see the forest for the trees" and find your way to a clearing.

Close your eyes and imagine yourself inside a dense forest. You are looking for a way out. You have been searching for a long time. All the trees look the same.

You find a fallen tree and sit down on it to rest and think of a new strategy. Suddenly your attention is drawn to a large tree in front of you. It is a beautiful tree, majestic and very old. It is a Tree of Knowledge. You become aware that it wishes to communicate with you.

The tree tells you that there is a solution to your dilemma. There is a way out of the forest. You listen carefully as the tree tells you where to find a path. You thank the tree for its help and, following the instructions, you find the path and are able to leave the forest.

At the edge of the forest is a beautiful clearing. You feel wonderful as you enter the clearing. All of the twists and turns and darkness of the forest have been left behind. You turn and look at the forest. Before, it was a maze of trees. Now you can see it and the trees within it with great clarity.

Standing in the clearing, you are warmed by the sun's light, which brings illumination to you. You realize that you now know exactly what to do. What are the impressions that are presented to you?

Recenter yourself and open your eyes. Write down your impressions. Perhaps a solution has been made obvious to you. Or, use free association to obtain more information from your impressions.

Use your imagination and psychic sense to create other exercises in which you "get the message."

Body wisdom

The body is one of our best psychic sensors. You already know from your own experience, and from your practice of the Keys, that you receive many signals through your body.

Your body also is your last line of defense when you fail to recognize other signals that something may not be right for you. It has been well-documented that stress is a major factor in many health issues. When we are stressed, the body speaks plainly back. And, if we do not honor our gifts and talents, thus creating an imbalance in our life, our bodies will speak up about that, too.

People who pay attention to their psychic power learn to listen to their bodies as well. Everyone has his or her unique talents and purpose in the world. When we are in harmony with that, our bodies function well. When we are out of harmony, our bodies tell us so.

Think of all the ways that language uses the body to describe negative emotional and psychic reactions:

- "He is a pain in the neck."
- "This makes me sick to my stomach."
- "I'm breaking my back to get this done."
- "This assignment is a major headache."
- "I'm knocked flat."
- "I'm paralyzed to do anything."

You may have noticed that when something is not appropriate for you, you receive an signal via your body. Sometimes this signal is a significant distress. Christiane Northrup, author of *Women's Bodies, Women's Wisdom,* noted that one of her medical student friends who had a "bad back" always experienced a flair-up of pain when she had to do something she did not want to do:

> Currently, she is contemplating writing a research paper. Whenever she thinks about writing this piece and the colleagues with whom she will be involved, she gets neck

pain and feels sick to her stomach. All her training has taught her that publishing this research paper is what she should do for her career. Yet her inner guidance, which speaks to her through her body's feeling, is telling her something quite different. She knows that she must take the radical step of choosing between her inner guidance and what society is telling her is best if she is to remain healthy.

Note the conflict between the body intuition and the rational mind's "should." We do this all the time, telling ourselves why we "must" or "should" do something that we clearly do not wish to do, or is not in our best interests. Even when our body tells us differently, we often ignore it, treating the symptoms instead of the cause.

Resolve to pay more attention to how your body speaks to you. Relate your body talk to your true feelings and emotions. Take appropriate action. It is not always possible to remove yourself entirely from a situation or relationship. However, there is always something you can do to bring yourself into better balance.

9

Problem Solving and Decision Making

Problems that defy solutions are vexing and can undermine self-confidence. The number one rule for psychic power problem-solving is to relax and know that for every problem there is the perfect solution.

Always approach problems from the highest perspective, not the lowest. If you are mired in mud you will not see the brilliance of the sky.

We are often called to make decisions in which the various options are neither obviously right nor wrong. Each option has its good points and its bad points. Which is the better or best way? Without the psychic input, we can go round and round in circles. Try these exercises when you feel stuck.

First, write up short summaries of each of your options, and list their advantages and disadvantages. Also list your honest thoughts and feelings about each one. Give a title to each option.

Exercise #1: Free Association

Free association exercises are often used in all kinds of settings to encourage creative and innovative breakthroughs. Use free association in all of these practical application exercises in this book.

Free association is simple. For example, let's say that your psychic sense gives you a symbol, a visual image, or a word or phrase. Write it down on a piece of paper. What else does it make you think of? Jot down your impressions quickly. Do not stop to think about them or analyze them. You will do that later. Your first impressions will give rise to secondary impressions. Record those as well. Soon you will have mapped out quite a few associations.

Continue with the free associations for as long as the energy carries you. Perhaps you will stop when you get a burst of insight that makes everything fall into place. Free associations often reveal to us our true thoughts and feelings. Analyze them and see what they have to tell you.

Exercise #2: Brainstorming Outside the Box

When you get buried in difficulties, it is hard to sort through everything. You are under pressure to make decisions, but nothing seems clear. You become afraid of making the wrong decisions. Result: paralysis.

Psychic power is a sharp blade that cuts through mental and emotional clutter.

The first step in problem-solving is to look for the most obvious and viable solutions, a process that engages the rational mind. Then look beyond, especially if there are no obvious solutions. Using free association, allow ideas to arise spontaneously and without judgment on feasibility and practicality. Sometimes the most unlikely suggestion leads to the hit that provides the solution. In a group think tank, participants speak out whatever comes to mind. If you are brainstorming outside the box by yourself, jot ideas down in a list. Hold nothing back.

Compose a clear question about the problem that needs to be solved. Finish one or more of these sentences in as many ways as possible:

- In my wildest dreams I would like...
- If anything were possible, then...
- If money were no object, then...
- In a perfect world...
- I would live happily ever after if...

Exercise #3: Fork in the Road

Close your eyes and see yourself traveling down a straight road. Whether you are walking or riding, you are proceeding carefully.

You come to a place where the road forks. There are as many branches of the road as there are options before you. From left to right, name the forks in the road with the titles of your options.

One by one, look down each fork. Notice the appearance of the roads. Are they well maintained, or are they filled with ruts and holes? What is the condition of the surrounding environment? Is the road in a desolate place or does it go through attractive scenery? Is the road straight, curved, or hilly?

Now take notice of your thoughts and feelings about the forks. Does one attract you while another repels you? Does one looks safe, and another dangerous?

What other details do you notice about each fork in road?

Reassess your options, using both your logical analysis and your psychic impressions.

Exercise #4: At the Crossroads

This exercise is useful for situations involving major changes in direction in life, such as changing jobs or careers, moving to a new city, getting married or divorced, undertakings that require a major commitment of time, energy and resources, and so on.

Draw up lists of the pros and cons about the situation. Then list your hopes and fears. Take a piece of paper and draw a crossroads intersection. The road you have been traveling on is at the bottom of the vertical. It represents what is behind you, and also the current road. The road at the top of the vertical cross represents the continuation of your present journey if you make no changes. To your right is the road that represents the change that you are considering. To your left is a mystery road—another direction unknown or not yet explored.

Close your eyes and imagine that you are traveling on a straight road. You arrive at the crossroads and stop. You have the option of continuing in the same direction, or taking a new road to the right or left. Which will it be?

As in the previous exercise, examine each road. How do their appearances and surrounding environments compare? What are your thoughts and feelings? Can you see your hopes or fears down any road?

Look carefully at the road on the right. When you feel you have examined it thoroughly, look at the road on the left. This is the unknown. It may represent an alternative that you have not considered. It may also represent information that you have overlooked. What do you see? Accept whatever arises spontaneously to you.

Do not be alarmed if the road on the left remains dark. It means that nothing new wishes to present itself.

Meditation exercises such as these often have a way of taking on their own life. For example, you might find yourself approached by a personification of your Inner Guide, who gives you a message or instructions, or who engages you in conversation. Or, you might be approached by other people who are involved in the decision. Allow your inner vision to unfold. You are not obliged to stick to any script. Trust that you will receive what you need.

Exercise #5: A Spiritual Approach

In his classic book *The Power of Positive Thinking*, minister and motivator Norman Vincent Peale told of the numerous politicians, leaders, and business persons he knew, many of them super achievers, who often turned to prayer in order to obtain guidance in problem-solving and decision-making. The great motivator Dale Carnegie would leave his office when times were busiest and most pressured and would visit a nearby church, where he sat quietly in prayerful meditation. Such a break stills the mind and enables needed insight to come through.

Questions to Ask Yourself

Here are suggestions to help you frame questions for solving problems and making decisions:

- What is the best solution/decision for me/for everyone?
- How can I implement the solution?
- What are the obstacles to a solution?
- Should I follow Plan A?
- When is the best time to _____ ?

10

Finding Your Purpose and Achieving Goals

Finding one's purpose in life ranks high on the list of reasons why people seek psychic consultations. Sooner or later, everyone wonders if he or she is pursuing the right career. Sooner or later, people feel stuck in their jobs or at a dead end and wonder what else they should do. Uncertainty about the direction of one's life always occurs during times of major change: loss of a job, death of a loved one, divorce, children leaving home, accidents and illness, and other upsets.

People often think that in order to find their true purpose they have to wipe the slate clean and make a radical change. Sometimes that is the case, but it is not always the best answer for everyone. Finding your true purpose can come through a hobby or a volunteer activity, or a change in the duties of your present job. A change in perspective can change your life as well. For example, I have met many people who suddenly feel called to become healers. They think that the way to accomplish this is to quit their job and open a retreat center in the mountains. Usually they have not thought through the practical business end, such as how they are going to arrange financing, run the facility, attract customers, and handle the day-to-day administrative matters.

There are many ways to become the healer, for example. You can take classes to learn a variety of energy healing modalities that will enable you to do healing as a lay practitioner. You can volunteer for a hospital, nursing home or hospice.

More important, however, is a shift in perspective to seeing that healing begins at home and in daily life. No matter what we do, we can aspire to bring healing energy to it. If you want to change "the system," don't abandon it. Work from within it to change it for the better.

Building your inner road maps

Realizing your highest potential and dreams is accomplished with the help of inner road maps built by psychic guidance. Your psychic power will help you see clearly where you are going and where you want to go (often the two are not the same). You will receive course corrections when the timing is right, thus avoiding delays and recovery time. And, your psychic sense will show you just how rich your path through life is: there are many possibilities and many choices.

Exercises

Exercise #1: Going to Ground Zero

Time is a great motivator to get priorities in order. Our time on this planet is finite, but we often live like we have endless time. We may in fact know what it is that we want to do, but we put it off while we do other things. Our life becomes full of "whens": "When such-and-such happens, then I will..." We convince ourselves, and anyone who will listen, that when the timing and circumstances are perfect, we will make our move.

Perfect circumstances seldom, if ever, arrive. If you are waiting for perfect, it's not going to happen.

If you were told that you had only one more year to live, what would you do? Would you stay in your job, stay in your marriage, continue to live in the home you don't like? Or would you go to "ground zero" and do what would matter to you most?

For this exercise, assume that you have one year left and money is no object. Take a piece of paper and list all of the things that you would do. Then list all of the things that you would let go. In both lists, circle the things that elicit your strongest emotions.

Now take another sheet of paper and list all of the obstacles that stand in your way: fears, practical matters, beliefs and so on. Take them one by one and write down why they are reasonable or why they are not.

Finally, list your solutions. What actions can you take to remove your obstacles? Ask your psychic power for help. Do free associations with your impressions.

Develop and implement a plan of action.

Exercise #2: Setting Goals

In order to reach a goal, you have to know your starting place. This requires an honest self-assessment. Take a sheet of paper and write down your goal. Be very specific. Then make a statement about where you are now. Be candid about your thoughts and feelings. Are you really ready to reach for your goal? Are you prepared to make the necessary changes, and even sacrifices? For example, you are not going to attract wealth if money runs through your fingers. You will have a hard time finding your ideal partner if you don't have a lot to offer yourself. And you will not get your degree if you don't enrolled in a program and study.

Close your eyes and ask your psychic power for guidance on how to get from point A to point B. Record your impressions and interpret them. You can also ask for a time line, such as how long it will take you to accomplish your goal.

Develop and implement a plan of action.

Do not overlook smaller daily goals, for they are just as important as long-range goals.

Exercise #3: Create the Future You Want

Super achievers do not wait for events—they make events happen. What do you want your future to bring? What would you like to be doing a year from now, five years from now, ten or more? Draw up a list of everything you would like to see come to pass in your relationships, career, home, health, and interests. Be bold. You have the power to set forces in motion that will help you achieve your dreams.

With the help of your psychic power, set your goals and objectives. Visualize yourself as already accomplishing them now. Create affirmations to support your goals. Impress your thoughts every day with your visualizations and affirmations. Believe in them, and act as though you have reached your goal.

"The man who assumes success tends already to have success," said Norman Vincent Peale. "People who assume failure tend to have failure. When either failure or success is picturized it strongly tends to actualize in terms equivalent to the mental image pictured."

For Peale, the formula was simple: Prayerize, Picturize, Actualize. He would pray for guidance about everything in life. When he felt clear on a goal, he built a mental picture of it already accomplished. He believed with all his might that it would come to pass, and that God would help him accomplish the goal. Then he acted as though the outcome had already happened. And, he did whatever he could to help bring the goal into reality.

Actor Jim Carrey, who became one of the highest-paid actors in Hollywood, pulled himself up from obscurity after writing himself a check for $10 million and proclaiming that it was his earnings. It was a powerful image, and Carrey, believing in himself, worked hard to make it come true. In fact, when he became a star he earned far more than $10 million for a single movie.

Expect the best and you will get the best.

If you are having difficulties with your self-confidence, then you should use visualizations and affirmations to build yourself up. Bolstering your faith in yourself may take time and effort, but the payoff is well worth the investment. Here are some tips that will help you:

- Everyone excels at something. What are your strengths and talents? Build powerful visualizations of your excellence. See yourself being recognized and appreciated by others. Change your behavior: act as though you are indeed worthy of respect and admiration.

- Extend your excellence to new areas. Don't be afraid to try something new. Ralph Waldo Emerson advised, "Do the thing you fear, and the death of fear is certain." Even if you do not succeed at first, you will gain in self-confidence.

- Remember that whatever you are doing now, you are capable of much more.

Exercise #4: Give Yourself the Green Light

You can make productive use of that time spent waiting at red traffic lights. While the light is red, focus on a goal you wish to obtain. When the light turns green, congratulate yourself on obtaining the goal.

Exercise #5: Give Yourself a Psychic Reading

We tend to believe what we are told, especially by authority figures. Such words create images and attitudes that become impressed upon us for better or for worse. For example, the placebo effect has been well documented in scientific studies: people who strongly believe they have been given an effective medication will react accordingly, even if they have been given only a sugar pill.

People sometimes seek out a psychic in the hopes of having their questions answered about what they should do and what will happen to them. A good reading can help the client obtain valuable insight. You should make your own decisions, however, and not expect a consultant to make them for you.

Try your own self-directed reading. You play the role of both client and psychic. The reading will fuel your visualizations and affirmations for success. It will tap into your psychic wisdom and clarify things.

Write out a list of questions to ask in the reading. Then assume the role of the reader and give answers. Tell yourself how wonderful you are, and that you are going to achieve your objectives. Allow whatever arises spontaneously to be your guidance. Put as much positive energy as you can into your reading.

When you are done, meditate for a while, holding vivid mental images of your "predictions" coming true.

Be sure to tape record your reading so that you can listen to it again and keep the energy flowing.

Exercise #6: Letters From Above

A variation of the self-directed psychic reading can be done in journaling, by writing letters to yourself from God, spiritual figures, saints, or angels. Address the letters to you personally, such as, "Dear Marie, This is your guardian angel speaking. ..." Deliver answers to questions and guidance. Allow your writing to flow freely and spontaneously—remember that the first thoughts are the best. This is a form of automatic writing, which is a way to access your psychic power, Higher Self, divine guidance, and deep creativity.

Try a "Letter From Above" on a regular basis. Reread your letters to keep the positive thoughts flowing. Over time, you will be able to track changes and growth.

Questions to Ask Yourself

Here are examples of questions to ask your psychic sense concerning your life's purpose and goals:

- What is my highest purpose in life?
- What are the obstacles that prevent me from attaining my highest potential?
- How can I fulfill my dreams?
- Is (Plan A) right for me?
- What is the best timing for me to implement (Plan A)?
- Where can I find the help and support I need to realize (Plan A/my goals)?

11

Increasing Your Prosperity

Using psychic power to make investment decisions is more widespread than you might think. Numerous articles have been published in which brokers, financial planners, and business executives reveal anonymously that they consult psychics, dreams, psychic tools, and astrology as aids in making their decisions.

I know many such people, both financial experts and novices. After realizing the power of his psychic sense, Brian, a financial novice, decided to try using it to make money in the stock market. For three months, he did nothing but study the market. Then he set goals. Every day, he did exercises to obtain guidance. Within a year he had made enough money to buy his dream vacation home at the beach.

It was not an entirely smooth ride, however, for there were losses and well as gains. "I feel that my intuition made a crucial difference," Brian said. "Without it, I think my dream home would be still a dream instead of a reality."

Psychic/intuitive investing is a practice with a successful history. For example, the American tycoon Cornelius Vanderbilt made a profit in gold shortly after the Civil War by consulting spirit guides for advice.

Vanderbilt wanted to capitalize on a fight for control of the gold market. In 1869, he consulted a medium, Victoria Woodhull, whose spirit guides told him to buy gold at $132 an ounce. Already a wealthy man, Vanderbilt followed the advice and invested $9.5 million. Speculation drove the price of gold up. Who knew where it would stop? Vanderbilt knew that when a market is over-heated by speculation, the price can plunge as rapidly as it can rise. To make the biggest profit, you have to know the right moment to bail out.

Woodhull told him she had a vision of the number 151, along with a gold bubble bursting. Vanderbilt sold at $150 an ounce, making $1.3 million in profits. The price of gold then plummeted.

Please be advised: as in all investments, do not jeopardize your financial security by putting at risk your entire savings. The exercises discussed here are for purposes of experimentation. None is risk-free. Results vary considerably. Remember that your psychic sense shows a *probable* future based on forces in motion. Markets are volatile, responding to many forces in motion.

Knowledge plus psychic power

You can get psychic hits about investments without detailed knowledge of the markets. However, if you are serious about psychic investing, you will increase your success if you also educate yourself about the marketplace. Information is the raw material of psychic sense. Your psychic power is an organizer of information and insight in bold, new ways. Successful financial planners and brokers are by nature psychic/intuitive, whether they realize it or not. They develop their own personal mechanisms for sensing deals, trends, and especially timing.

Make your commitment and tell your psychic mind that you wish it to present you with investment advice. Set specific goals. What do you wish to accomplish, and in what time frame? Put your commitment and goals in motion with meditation, affirmations, and dream incubation instructions. Make a commitment also to act on your guidance, just as you do in other matters in life. What are you willing to do to help realize these goals? You might vow to spend a certain amount of time each day attending to your finances, or to increase your capacity for risk-taking.

Getting the right information

Intuitive consultant Nancy Rosanoff recommends to "gather information intuitively" and "gather intuitive information." Use your psychic power to increase your knowledge of the field. It is important to familiarize yourself with the language and landscape of investing. Let your psychic sense guide you to the sources right for you. Then, use your skill to help you make decisions from your knowledge.

Brian, mentioned at the beginning of this chapter, devoted three months to study before making a single investment. During his "psychic apprenticeship," he made practice investments without using actual money, and then tracked his results. This enabled Brian, a conservative man, to gain confidence in his investing abilities and sharpen his skill without putting any of his funds at risk.

Select any of the exercises in this book to help you frame questions and explore the financial territory. You may discover that information starts coming to you in dreams. Nurture this source by paying more attention to your dreams, and asking yourself questions for your dreams to answer.

Dispel fear

Sometimes psychic guidance runs counter to prevailing wisdom and trends. You might receive guidance to sell when everyone else is still buying, such as what happened to Cornelius Vanderbilt. Or, you might feel strongly about buying when there is no concrete evidence that a particular stock is going to perform well. Only your experience over time will teach you how to heed your guidance.

Beware of fear. Investing is not for the fearful under any circumstances. Fear impedes the psychic flow and leads to poor choices. You can head off fear by practicing detachment from results. Affirm every day that you invest with confidence.

In the Keys exercises for Meditation Adventures, you learned how to remain detached from thoughts, and how to release thoughts as they arise. Practice this with fear as well. If you feel yourself in the grip of fear, gently release it and replace it with light.

If you make a mistake, review how it happened and what you can learn from it, and move forward.

Associative remote viewing

As part of your psychic investment exploration, try an exercise called "associative remote viewing," so-named in parapsychological research. It requires at least three persons, and can be done as a group project. Perhaps you are in an investment club or circle that might like to give it a try.

Associative remote viewing involves looking into the future for specific events by association. The procedure was developed by researchers Russell Targ, Stephen Schwartz, and Ed May. It works like this:

Simple objects such as a ball or piece of fruit are assigned to several possible future events. For example, the project involves Stock A. A ball represents buy, a stick represents sell, a briefcase represents hold. One person serves as the viewer, who does *not* know either the project (such as a specific stock) or the chosen objects. The viewer looks into the future to see which object will be placed in his hands or presented to him on a certain date. Let's say the viewer looks ahead one month and sees a stick, or an object that is stick-like. The viewer reports his results to an interviewer, who also does not know the particulars of the project or the objects, either. It is important that both viewer and interviewer do not subconsciously interpret results.

The interviewer reports his findings to the investors, who then gauge that in one month, it will be an optimum time to sell Stock A.

Does it work? Results with controlled experiments have varied.

In 1982, the researchers conducted a now-famous associative remote viewing experiment with a renowned remote viewer, Keith Harary, on the silver futures market. A group of anonymous investors bought and sold futures according to the objects perceived by Harary, who was working "blind." The objects included a vial of perfume, a pair of eyeglass frames and a plastic bag of washers. More than $100,000 profit was made.

The group fell apart and some litigation resulted. The next year, a subsequent experiment to replicate the results failed. Years later, Targ tried another replication with others and succeeded, but without profit.

Why are money issues different than other issues when it comes to using psychic power?

The spirituality of money

The researchers were not the only ones who experience hit-and-miss results when it comes to psychic power and money. Many people who have contacted me report similar results: psychic investment can pay off, sometimes handsomely, but it can also produce losses. When people make the commitment to stay the course, however, they feel their gains outweigh their losses.

Why is it that our psychic sense can work spectacularly well except when it comes to money?

One reason has to do with the nature of numbers themselves. As Targ has pointed out, numbers are abstracts, and it is often difficult for the psychic mind to grasp abstracts.

Another reason is, as I pointed out earlier, investing involves the confluence of many minds which are in constant collision in their objectives.

A major reason has to do with our collective feelings about money. We carry a lot of guilt about wanting money and having money. Our spiritual and religious traditions teach us that desire for money is greed and attachment to the material is "unspiritual."

Spiritual teachers on down through the ages have told us that one must never use spiritual or paranormal powers for personal gain, especially. When one becomes empowered through spiritual study and practice, one should turn to service, not profit. And yet, without making money, nothing much would be accomplished in terms of innovation, commerce, technology, and services.

No wonder we have a subconscious schizophrenic discomfort over money. This is particularly evident in the New Age or "spiritual living" arena, where people who wish to earn their living as healers, readers, self-empowerment facilitators and so on are criticized for charging fees for their services. The same critics have no problem paying doctors, lawyers, accountants, and other service providers their fees, however.

What is the "right" answer is to the philosophical questions about money? Like everything else in life, you must find your own truth and comfort zone about it. Do not let others impose their values on you.

It is our spiritual birthright to be whole and happy, and to live to our fullest potential. Our psychic power is a natural gift to help us fulfill our birthright. If you wish to use your power to increase your wealth, then do so, and strive to find the right balance for it in how you live your life and apply your wealth.

Questions to Ask Yourself

Set your financial course with the following questions:

- What are the best ways to accomplish my financial goals?
- Is _____ the right financial advisor for me?
- When is the best time to _____ (buy/sell/hold)?
- Is this the right _____ (fund, stock, bond, investment, etc.) for me?
- Should I _____ now? Where can I find the best sources of data/information that I need?

12

Improving Your Relationships

Your psychic power will help you build and maintain better relationships at home, work, in social life, and in daily life. If you are not getting along well with someone, your psychic sense can tell you why and what to do about it, and even the best time to take action. It will help you find ways to build trust and cooperation, and deepen intimacy. It will help you zero in on the best business prospects and sources of help.

Exercise #1: Making the Most of Gatherings and Events

When I attend a social gathering, I first set a goal. If it is business oriented, my goal might be to meet the right person(s) for a project, or gain the support or interest of someone in particular. If it is a social event, my goal might be to meet a person knowledgeable about a certain subject, or a person with whom I can form a mutually prosperous and fulfilling friendship. Or, I might want to just enjoy myself.

It is important to enter a gathering with a purpose set in your mind. Otherwise, you will be at the mercy of other people's intentions. Some of them may have nothing more in mind than aimlessly passing their time and wasting yours.

For example, I attended a networking event of authors, freelance writers, editors and others in publishing. My goal: to meet an editor who would buy an idea I wished to write about. Many of the people were strangers to me.

I asked my psychic sense to show me the person, or persons, whom I should approach to accomplish my goal. As I cast my eye around the room, I was strongly drawn to a woman not far from me. I heard the words "that one" in my inner ear, accompanied by a confirming, expansive sensation in the solar plexus.

I made an opportunity to introduce myself. I didn't jump on her with my idea, but got around to it in the course of talking about her interests. "Isn't that amazing," she said. "I happen to be looking for someone right now who can write about..." What a "coincidence"! I made an appointment to follow up, and two weeks later I had a deal.

Perhaps I would have met her sooner or later, but in a large room full of people, I might have spent the entire evening talking to many people, but not the "right" ones.

You can use your psychic radar in similar circumstances to identify sales prospects, influential persons, news sources, financial sources, romantic prospects, and so on, as well as people to avoid.

Prior to an event, make a clear statement about your goal. What do you wish to leave the event having accomplished?

Ask your psychic radar to give you unmistakable sign to help you navigate through the crowd and find the people you need to accomplish your goal.

Give thanks for your success.

Exercise # 2: Finding a Romantic Partner

Everyone wants to find a partner who is well-matched and right. Some people only have to search once; most look again and again as a change of heart, divorce, or loss create new circumstances. Your psychic power can help you in the search for your ideal partner or soulmate, someone who matches your emotional, physical, intellectual, and spiritual needs.

Using psychic free association, compose a portrait of your ideal partner. List the traits, qualities and characteristics you desire. In another list, state how you would complement those attributes. List everything about you that you would bring to a new relationship.

Now turn your psychic sense into a beacon or searchlight that will help you find this person. Everything in the universe is energy. The energy can assume any form, and become organized into patterns, such as the physical realm. Matter is energy. Consciousness is energy. Our thoughts and feelings are energy. Creativity is energy. The essence of the soul is energy.

The energies of the universe are in constant motion and interplay. As energies affect each other, they change form. In this fashion, our "reality" is created. We are co-creators of our reality, making it and changing it by what we think, say and do.

The universe is a mighty current of energy that represents the whole. It constantly moves toward a state of perfection, which is harmony and balance of the whole. Soulmates are an expression of that harmony, balance, and wholeness.

The following exercise, "The Golden Stream," will set the intention with your psychic mind to be in a "perfect flow" and draw to you the circumstances in which you will meet your new partner:

> Imagine yourself floating down a gentle river. Notice that the water is golden. The sunlight falling upon it makes the surface sparkle like millions of golden gems. You are warm, happy and content, floating easily down the river. You are fully present to the moment. There is no past, no tomorrow, only the eternal moment.
>
> The gems sparkle and flash. The river of water becomes a river of light.
>
> As you float along in the river of light, become aware of your body. It begins to change. See yourself being filled by the golden light of the sun, and by the sparkles from the river. The light transforms you, turning you into a golden being. You become lighter and lighter. You see that the golden light that is now you is actually comprised of millions of sparkling golden gem lights, just like the sunlight dancing on the water of the river. Allow yourself to sink deeper and deeper into this field of sparkling lights. You feel energized. Suddenly you realize that you are one and the same with the river of light.

Feel the flow of the motion of light. Allow yourself to be carried along with it. You are filled with complete peace and harmony, at one with the light.

Up ahead you see a round, golden ball of light. It is the Source of All Being, the supply of universal good. The river of light is flowing into it. A cosmic river merging into a cosmic sun. The golden sun is your desire, which is your union with your ideal partner. The river flows effortlessly into it, merging perfectly with it.

Feel yourself merging with the energy of your partner. It becomes part of you, and you become part of it. You cannot be separated from it. Stay in this space for a few moments, and notice how you feel.

When you feel ready, return to an awareness of your physical body. As you feel more solid, know that the light remains within you. The connection to all which is yours.

Questions to Ask Yourself

Your psychic power will come to your aid for any matter in a relationship. Whether it is a problem at home or a problem at work, your psychic sense can help smooth the course. Are you in a confrontation? Your psychic sense instantly will tell you what to say or do to defuse the situation.

Your power can also tell you where or how to find a new partner, and whether a romantic relationship is on the right course. It is not uncommon to project desires onto relationships, and thus fail to see shortcomings. Your psychic power will keep you clear-eyed and level-headed.

Using any of the techniques in this book, ask your power to help you with questions such as these:

- What is the reason for the problem with_____?
- How can I resolve my difference with _____?
- When is the best time to _____?

- How can I _____? (Improve my relationship with someone, get better cooperation, get approval for a project, etc.)
- Is my relationship with _____ right for me?
- How can I find the partner who is right for me?
- Where can I find the partner who is right for me?
- Will this relationship _____ (survive/end/change, etc.)? How can I motivate _____ to _____?
- What should I say now?
- How can I help _____ with _____?

13

Enhancing Your Creativity, Health and Self-Improvement

Once it is encouraged to blossom, your psychic power will be a constant source of inspiration and creativity, from ways to make daily life better to ways to change direction in life.

Pay special attention to your ideas, no matter how far-fetched they seem, and keep a record of them. Every idea actually is a glimpse of a real future, one that you have the power to manifest, provided your faith and efforts stay on course. When you let good ideas die out of lack of action, you let a future die with them. Inspired ideas are gifts of the psychic power—a vision of a future that can be yours.

Here are some exercises I have found useful in my own life. In particular, "A Pen in the Hand of God" and "Walking the Labyrinth" can be done again and again, and always yield fresh treasures.

Exercise #1: A Pen in the Hand of God

One morning, I sat down in my room to meditate as part of my custom of opening the day's activities. I had a visionary experience that resulted in this exercise that establishes a connection to a divine source of inspiration.

Play some gentle meditation music in the background. Allow the music to relax you. Now read the following text out loud in a slow and measured voice. Or, as an alternative, record the text at an earlier time. For the meditation, play the music and text together, and close your eyes while you listen.

I am a pen in the hand of God.
I stand in the Temple of Eternal Light. Before me is the Book of Life.
The Book of Life is the record of everything that a soul thinks, says and does. All impulses and acts of consciousness stand written in its pages forever. My acts of compassion. My unkind words. My generosity. My selfishness. My love. My anger. My happiness. My sadness. And so it goes.
I look at the Book of Life. It shimmers gold and white. Its numberless pages go back to before time began, and extend into infinite timelessness.
The Book of Life is tended by angels who are the record-keepers of the soul's journey to God. They tend to the book without prejudice, without judgment, and with love. They serve God, and they serve the soul in its quest to unite with God. The angels sing constant praises to God. They sing encouragement to the souls who are the living expressions of God.
The angels show me that there are no mistakes in the Book of Life. Only lessons. Some lessons are easy. Some are hard. Sometimes many chapters are written before a single lesson is learned.
What will I write in the Book of Life today? I am a pen in the hand of God.
Will I write that I act out of love? Or will I write that I act out of thoughtlessness?
Thoughtlessness keeps me separated from God. Love brings me into Oneness with God.
Before I write in the Book of Life today, I ask:
What does God wish to write?
The answer arises within my heart:
"Bring Truth, Beauty, Harmony and Love into the world."
I am a pen in the hand of God.

Now write in your journal. Write quickly and without judgment—words, ideas, inspirational pieces, poetry, letters to friends and loved ones, personal feelings—whatever seeks expression.

Enhancing Your Creativity, Health and Self-Improvement

I do "A Pen in the Hand of God" whenever I need to refresh my energy, tap a vein of creativity, and restore spiritual balance.

Exercise #2: The Inner Alarm

Your psychic power is a watchdog that never sleeps, whose vision is not limited by distance. You can instruct your psychic power to watch out for the well-being of anyone or anything. This exercise was inspired by the experience of Harold Sherman, one of the early pioneers of ESP research.

One night Sherman and his wife entertained dinner guests at their New York City apartment. When the guests left, they discovered that thieves have broken into their automobile and stolen some new clothing.

That night Sherman meditated on this. He gave his psychic power these instructions: *"No one ever will attempt to steal anything of mine and that I will be made aware of the theft in time to prevent it!"* He repeated this affirmation until he felt it take hold within his subconscious. He then released it from his conscious mind.

A year later, Sherman met a friend at a restaurant for dinner in New York. He hung his plain, gray overcoat on an open rack and took a table about fifty feet away. He was engaged in an animated conversation with suddenly his inner voice said, *"Quick! That man has your overcoat!"* He commented in *How to Make ESP Work for You*:

> I look toward the coat rack just as a man had taken a coat from it and was putting it on as he headed toward the cashier's desk. There were perhaps twenty coats on the rack and a number of them, at that distance, look as though they could have been mine. But now, trained to follow my hunches, I found myself on my feet, cutting through between the tables. En route, my Conscious Mind began to get its licks at me. "Be careful!" it warned. "If you accuse this man of taking your overcoat, and he doesn't have it, you can get yourself in trouble!"
>
> I weighed this warning against my inner feeling and my inner feeling won out.

Sherman informed the man that he had taken his coat. The man vehemently denied it. Fortunately, Sherman had papers in its pockets that positively identified him as the owner of the coat. The man apologized and handed him back his coat, saying that it looked like his own. The man took a few steps as though to return to the coat rack and then bolted out the door. Clearly, he had intended to steal the coat.

Note how Sherman paid attention to his psychic power twice. The first time came when he had the sudden impression that the man had taken his coat. Then his rational mind interfered, suggesting that it might be a mistake. Sherman did not allow this to overrule his psychic power.

Also note that once Sherman had given the watchdog instructions to his psychic power, and they stayed in force even though a long time elapsed before they were needed. And, Sherman didn't have the slightest worry about the safety of his overcoat when he met his friend for dinner. Yet he received a warning loud and clear as soon as a situation violated his instructions to his psychic power. This demonstrates the incredible power of the psychic power to serve us in times of need an emergency.

Sherman stressed that it is very important to give ourselves the correct instructions, otherwise we will get the wrong result. Instructions, or affirmations, should be worded to reflect the results we desire, not the results we fear. Said Sherman:

> If I had feared that I would, someday, be the victim of a theft, and had I strongly pictures this possibility, this would have been the same as ordering my higher faculties of mind to create a susceptibility in me for such a happening. Under such conditions, it is not likely that my mind would have reacted in a way to protect me, as it so obviously did in conformance with my prior instruction.

How would you like your psychic power to be your all-seeing watchdog for you? We know from our exercises in expanded vision, expanded listing, and remote viewing that our consciousness can be sent to distant locations. You can ask your psychic power to protect your premises while you are away, guard your house while you sleep, watch your belongings, and protect the while you travel. This does not mean, of course, that you are then free to be careless or taken unnecessary risks. But your psychic power will be like an extra insurance policy.

Here are some affirmation instructions to activate your inner alarm, including the example given by Sherman:

- *No one will ever attempt to steal anything of mine but that I will be made aware of the theft in time to prevent it.*
- *If anyone attempts to break into my home or property, I will know it in time to prevent it.*
- *I will be alerted to any unsafe conditions in my travel in time to avoid them.*
- *I will be alerted to any threats to my personal safety in time to avoid them.*

In a meditative state, repeat one of these affirmations, or one you write to suit your specific needs, until you feel it is "locked" into consciousness. Sherman, who was very experienced using his psychic faculties, programmed his psychic power once. I find it useful to periodically refresh an affirmation.

Exercise #3: Walking the Labyrinth

The labyrinth is a walking meditation revered since ancient times for its transformative and healing powers. It is an archetypal mandala for a journey of consciousness, a search for knowledge and truth. Laid out on the ground or a floor, the labyrinth is entered and walked in a circular fashion to its center, and then exited by another circular route. When you walk the labyrinth, you experience a quieting of the mind, an opening of the heart, and an awakening of wholeness, oneness, and potential. The labyrinth inspires change from within a deep level of the self. You can experience a refreshing renewal that leads to peace of mind and clarity of thoughts. You can experience psychic flashes and breakthroughs.

The motif of the labyrinth has appeared for thousands of years in mythology, architecture, art, dance, rites, and rituals. The oldest surviving labyrinth, dating to circa 2500 BC, appears on a rock carving at Luzzanas on the island of Sardinia, Italy. Fragments of labyrinth designs can be traced back to 6500 BC. The Egyptians, Greeks, Celts and Indians made great use of labyrinths as well.

The term "labyrinth" is believed to come from *labrys*, or the double axe, a symbol of the Greek god Zeus. The double axe was the symbol of power in the Minoan culture in ancient Crete, where labyrinths were especially prevalent.

In the Middle Ages, the labyrinth became a walking substitute for the sacred pilgrimage to the Holy Land. During the wars of the Crusades, from the eleventh to thirteenth centuries, journeys to the Holy Land were dangerous. The Roman Catholic Church designated seven cathedral labyrinths in Europe as acceptable replacements that would offer the same spiritual renewal as an actual pilgrimage. Walking the labyrinth gave pilgrims the experience of communion with the ultimate reality: the knowledge of Self, and the knowledge that God and Self are one. The most famous labyrinth still remaining is on the floor of the Cathedral at Chartres, France.

With the advent of the Age of Science, labyrinths declined in importance m spiritual practice. In recent years, the labyrinth has been revived. People once again have connected with the power of the circular path a metaphor for the spiritual journey: all you have to do is follow the path and it will take you inward.

The labyrinth has no dead-ends and wrong turns, but has one path that leads to the center. Thus, it represents the mystery of the soul's journey to the Mystic Center. The path does not go directly to the center, but takes a meandering, circular route that enables the traveler to go through distinct shifts in consciousness along the way. From the center, the same path leads out. This represents the return to the world, in which the gifts of illumination are brought back to be manifested in life.

The labyrinth also symbolizes the journey of regeneration and enlightenment found in many religious traditions. In Christianity, this journey is called Union with God. In Buddhism it is the Path to Enlightenment, and in Hinduism the Path to Freedom.

You can find the nearest public labyrinths to you online. You can also find for sale portable labyrinths and finger labyrinths, for which you use your finger to "walk" the path.

In preparation for walking a labyrinth, compose a question to which you seek an answer. Address a significant matter. Be willing to accept whatever answers arise from your experience.

There are three stages to walking the labyrinth:

Stage 1: Entering the labyrinth. As you walk to the center, focus on the releasing, emptying, and quieting of negative thoughts. Relinquish the things you have sought to control and the worries which control you, and surrender yourself to the journey. If annoying thoughts keep intruding, gently release them; do not try to resist them or dismiss them. Travel the path slowly. Have no expectations, only an open mind and an open heart ready to receive the gifts of the labyrinth.

In mystical terms, this stage is called Purgation, which is the release of all things that block communication with the Higher Self. We cannot hear the inner voice when our minds are busy.

Stage 2: Entering the center. Many times reaching the center of the labyrinth comes as a surprise because of the winding, circular path. You don't know you're "there" until you're there, which reflects what oftentimes happens in life. The key to realizing life's potential is to be present to the moment. Only when you are present to the moment are you in contact with your full creative potential.

Once in the center of the labyrinth, linger for a moment, for it is here that breakthroughs in psychic power and creativity occur. The gifts of the labyrinth reveal themselves in startling clarity. They may include insight into a problem or situation; new perspectives; creative ideas; and feelings of empowerment, integration, receptivity, authenticity, and self-confidence.

In mystical terms, this stage is called Illumination, which is the knowing of the sacred self within.

Stage 3: Leaving the labyrinth. On the journey out, allow yourself to feel replenished, balanced, and empowered by your experience. Travel slowly to allow the new energies to take hold. Be absorbed in your self-revelation.

In mystical terms, this stage is called Union, which means communion with and being absorbed into God. You bring Truth into your being.

Following exit from the labyrinth, spend some quiet time in meditation and reflection to integrate the experience. Record your experience and insights in your journal.

Your experiences with the labyrinth will vary. Sometimes they will be profound. Other times, you might simply feel relaxed. Walking the Labyrinth is an alchemical process that continues to unfold. Like other forms of innerwork, the labyrinth opens one up to new flows of energies. Pay attention to dreams and synchronicities, which can bring more psychic information, wisdom and ideas. Daily prayer and meditation also augment the labyrinth experience.

Your Inner Health Advisor

Your Higher Self knows how to keep you balanced and centered. Inadequate sleep, wrong food, too much stress, too little exercise, and so on will put you out of balance. Intellectually, you know the remedies, but may ignore them.

Make it your daily habit to meditate. Meditation can greatly reduce stress, one of the major factors behind many health problems.

Instruct your psychic power to help you enhance and maintain health and well-being.

Janice could barely make it through a day without her energy flagging. She often found it hard to concentrate; sometimes she was easily irritated. She knew she was trying to juggle too much, but felt she had to maintain her activities. When she asked her inner health advisor for help, she received a mental impression of herself asleep. At first she thought it was a joke, her Higher Self telling her she was asleep at the wheel of life. The guidance clarified with these words: "Get more sleep."

An obvious answer, but impossible, Janice thought. In fact, she was thinking of cutting back on her nightly sleep in order to compensate for her lethargy during the day. She could accomplish a lot with an extra thirty minutes a day.

The inner guidance was insistent: "Get more sleep." She had the "feeling" that she really needed about an hour more than she was allowing herself. Losing an hour seemed unthinkable.

Janice finally decided to follow the guidance. She had no trouble at all sleeping an extra hour each night—her body seemed to drink up the additional sleep. She quickly realized an improvement in her well-being: in mood, energy, concentration, and vitality. To her surprise, she discovered that she was able to get more done in less time during the day. "I made the mistake of being ruled by statistics," she said. "I slept according to what I understood was 'average.' The truth is, I seem to need more sleep than most others. My psychic power called my attention to what my body was already trying to tell me."

Some years ago, I received a strong inner prompting to cut back on my exposure to daily news. I was in the habit of watching news shows in the morning, evening and prior to bed, plus whenever I happened to plunk down on the couch for a break from work.

Daily news is overwhelmingly bad: accidents, murders, political tension, scandals, disasters, and unhappy people. While it behooves us to stay reasonably informed about important events and developments, we do not need to know all the bad news that happens around the planet every day. Most of these events are beyond our control and sphere of influence. Listening to accounts of them is emotionally draining, and fosters a mindset of powerlessness. These negative effects can linger for a long time.

I found that when I cut back substantially on news shows, I experienced an overall lifting of stress and tension. I did not feel that I was in the dark, but in control of my own news feed.

Dr. Andrew Weil, in his book, *Spontaneous Healing*, recommends periodic "news fasts" as part of an overall good health program. He observes:

> By the way, a major source of my own mental turmoil is the news. The percentage of stories in the news that make me feel good is very small; the percentage of stories that make me feel anxious or outraged is very large and increasing, as new media focus more and more on murder, mayhem and misery. It is easy to forget that we have a choice as to whether we let this information into our minds and thoughts.

How else does our psychic power help us with health?

Our psychic power often gives us early warnings and advice about health matters. I have studied dreams for most of my life, and have found dreams to be an especially rich source of this kind of information. The diagnostic and healing powers of dreams have been known and used since ancient times around the world. Sometimes illness is forecast in dreams before obvious symptoms show up in the body. And, when we are injured or ailing, dreams sometimes help us with information that speeds our recovery. By paying attention to our dreams, we receive guidance that can help us to maintain good health.

In *The Power of the Mind to Heal*, Joan Borysenko recounts how dreams alerted her to a precancerous condition in her breast. In her dream, she was clutching a bottle of nitroglycerin over her right breast. She arrived at the hospital just in time for nurse to throw the nitroglycerin down the drain before it could explode. When she awakened, she could still feel a sensation of heat in her breast. After more breast dreams, she said, "I believed that the unconscious wisdom of the body might be trying to give me an important message."

Borysenko visited a doctor, who was skeptical that anything was wrong. She had no obvious lumps and her mammograms were clear except for a small calcium deposit. The doctor dismissed the dream and suggested she find a way to manage anxiety and cancer phobia.

Months later, reminded of the nitroglycerin dreams, Borysenko had the calcium deposit biopsied. It was diagnosed as precancerous and not yet malignant. She was relieved. "The 'nitroglycerin' was poured down the drain before it could explode," she said.

Experiences such as this are well documented in medical, psychotherapy, dream and self-help literature. I describe healing dreams in detail in *Dreamwork for Visionary Living*.

Our psychic power uses other ways to reach us about our health besides dreams. For example, in my book *Christmas Angels: True Stories of Hope and Healing*, I tell the story of a young man who discovered his own cancer after hearing a friend tell him about the same kind of cancer that had struck the friend's mother. The cancer was in the neck. As he heard the story, the young man felt an urge to rub his own neck–and felt a suspicious lump.

If your psychic power tugs at you concerning your health, pay attention. But please note: the psychic power is not a substitute for medical diagnosis or treatment, or other professional health care.

Questions to Ask Yourself

Here are questions to pose concerning your creativity, health, and self-improvement:

- How can I better develop my talent for _____?
- What new talents should I explore?

Enhancing Your Creativity, Health and Self-Improvement

- How can I increase my happiness and satisfaction in life?
- How should I improve/change my lifestyle?
- How can I heal _____?
- How can I attain and maintain my desired weight?
- How can I _____ (overcome bad habits, change behavior, etc.)?

14

Achieving Abundant Living

Perhaps your interest in psychic power started with a desire to make better decisions. Your psychic power will do that for you, but it will do much more. Your psychic power will make possible more abundant living. It will help you reach your goals and make your dreams come true.

I'd like to share a few final thoughts on happiness, fulfillment, and abundant living.

Master Affirmations

Your self-improvement plan should include the regular use of affirmations, which help to condition your psychic power—as well as your beliefs, thoughts and actions—to respond in desired ways. If you have been working with affirmations as part of the development plan set forth in this book, then you have already experienced their power to facilitate transformation and breakthroughs.

I have been a fan of the popular comic character *Dilbert*, a hapless engineer at the mercy of a dehumanized workplace. When a business executive friend of mine told me that Dilbert's creator, Scott Adams, had used affirmations to build his success, naturally I was intrigued. Scott's experiences are in his book, *The Dilbert Future: Thriving on Business Stupidity in the 21st Century*.

According to Scott, he tried affirmations on the recommendation of a friend. He neither believed in them nor disbelieved in them. He did not feel that they required any particular faith or positive thinking to work. He picked what he thought was a "very unlikely goal" and went to work on it, writing his affirmation fifteen times a day and visualizing it. Within a week, he experienced strings of amazing coincidences, and within a few months, the goal was accomplished.

He then tried an affirmation to "get rich in the stock market." He wrote the affirmation and waited for inspiration. One morning he awakened at 4 AM with the words "buy Chrysler" in his mind. The psychic hit came on the brink of a spectacular recovery of Chrysler stock (Scott did not buy the stock, however, due to difficulties in getting a brokerage account established.)

He tried again with stocks and received another accurate psychic hit about a company just going public, whose stock climbed rapidly. Scott made a small profit—the stock continued to rise after he sold it.

Scott turned affirmations toward other goals, all of which were successful. For example, he scored a ninety-fourth percentile on his exam to qualify for a master of business administration program. He became a successful syndicated cartoonist despite enormous odds against him. He turned *Dilbert* into "the most successful comic on the planet," realizing that goal when two of his *Dilbert* books rode the top of the *New York Times* bestseller list.

It is a fascinating account. However, I firmly believe that faith in the outcome and positive thinking are intrinsic to the success of affirmations. Affirmations do focus your intent and consciousness whether you are aware of it or not. Faith and positive thinking—and thus action—are conditioned in the process. If your commitment to a goal is vague or filled with doubt, affirmations are not likely to be successful.

I have used affirmations in all areas of life: relationships, health, success, creativity, and my spiritual path. They are wonderful tools for strengthening vision, determination, and perseverance, especially when energy flags and faith droops.

I always phrase my affirmations in the present tense: "I am..." "I have..." "I receive..." This creates the expectation that the goal is already obtained.

Remember to follow the five-step advice given in Chapter 4 about affirmations:

- 1. Create a clear affirmation.
- 2. Believe in every cell of your being that it is right for you.
- 3. See yourself as having achieved or attained your goal now.
- 4. Ask for guidance and help through your psychic power.
- 5. Do everything you can to create your new reality.

Do not overload your psychic power with too many affirmations at a time. Select two or three to work with over a period of a few months.

Here are twenty-two Master Affirmations that will enhance your self-confidence, self-empowerment, creativity, relationships, health and well-being, financial prosperity, and decision-making ability:

- I honor and use my special abilities and skills
- I have a unique and special contribution to make
- I accept prosperity and abundance into my life
- I trust that everything comes in the perfect time and in the perfect way
- I am open to receive with every breath that I take
- I am peaceful, relaxed and centered
- I trust myself
- I am lovable and loving
- I am beautiful and radiant

- I am enjoying excellent health and energy
- I am the master of my life
- I am whole and complete in myself
- I am in radiant health, filled with light and love
- I am happy and satisfied in my relationship with (name)
- I enjoy great financial prosperity
- I express original, creative ideas
- I make the right decisions
- I have plenty of energy for all that I choose to do
- I am beautiful, loving, and lovable
- I appreciate my body
- I am relaxed and centered
- I receive infinite riches that are now flowing freely into my life

Meditation exercises for affirmations

Use meditative visualization exercises to help the manifestation of all of your affirmations.

Select one of the affirmations for prosperous living, or write your own. Follow the procedures for Psychic Power Breathing and relaxation.

When you are ready, repeat the affirmation either aloud or silently. As you do so, build a vivid mental image of the affirmation. Let yourself star in it. Activate all your senses in the imagery. Make the picture as intense and vivid as possible.

Hold the image as long as you can.

Release the image. As you release it, give thanks for its manifestation in your life. Give thanks for having what you envision now.

Carry the image with you in your thoughts. Call it up often.

If you feel doubt, then examine why. Perhaps you don't feel you deserve what you seek. You must get to the root cause and correct it. Perhaps you need to reword the affirmation, or work with another one first.

Keep a record of your progress with affirmations. *Expect results*—you will get them.

Living abundantly

You now have a complete guide and plan for improving life in any area. Experiment with the techniques until you find the ones that resonate with you and produce the best results. Practice them and keep track of your results. Soon you will see patterns that will help you hone your skills even more.

After a while, psychically empowered living becomes part of the backdrop of daily life. Your attitudes, beliefs, expectations, and approaches to life change in both profound and subtle ways. The abundance that once seemed unattainable is achieved.

Appendix
Psychic Power Etiquette

Case: You are having a conversation with someone when suddenly you have psychic impressions about things that are going on in his or her life. You feel the urge to speak up. Should you?

Case: Someone finds out you are psychic and comes up to you and asks for a demonstration of your ability. Should you give one?

Case: Someone asks you to see into the future for them. Should you?

As you grow psychically, it is inevitable that you will be caught off guard in situations such as these unless you give some thought to your "psychic power etiquette." It may not always be appropriate to say what you sense.

Always keep in mind that your psychic power is a skill and a tool, not a toy. It should be used wisely. Here are some guidelines for sound psychic power habits.

Social settings

Speak by invitation only

In the course of daily interactions with people, you find yourself aware of their emotions or circumstances below the surface. Some of them might be troubling. Perhaps you also sense a solution to a problem or an outcome of a stressful situation. In the full blaze of your psychic glory, you blurt out, "I know you're worried about your daughter taking that trip by herself, but she's going to be fine." Or, "I think you should sell that piece of property." Or, perhaps you offer a well-intended inspirational boost: "There's no need to be so depressed about your finances—you have got a lot of good things going for you!" Rather than being showered with gratitude, you are met with reactions ranging from puzzlement to discomfort to irritation—even anger. Stung, you wonder why. You were only trying to help.

Your heart may have been in the right place, but you unwittingly intruded upon the other person's private space. Most people do not appreciate unsolicited advice no matter what the source. The demonstration that you know something personal that has not been broached verbally may also upset someone. While psychic power has made its way into many public arenas of thought, most people do not like the idea that others, especially casual acquaintances or strangers, may be able to see into their minds and their lives. Some persons may be truly frightened by it as well. At the very least, your advice may go unabsorbed, rolling off like water from a duck's back. Everyone moves through life at their own pace, and your unsolicited comments may be premature.

It is better to keep spontaneous psychic impressions to yourself. Let them become part of your overall understanding of someone else. File them away, and if the opportunity presents itself, make use of them when your views are invited.

There are times when exceptions are made to this rule. Speak up if your psychic power is strongly telling you to do so. You may be serving as a tool of divine intervention—a synchronicity in which someone hears what they need to hear in order to take action. You must be *very* clear about this, however, for it is all too easy to fall into the glamor that you are a walking tool of divine intervention all the time.

Sometimes psychic impressions provide valid warnings. Leah dreamed that something was wrong with one of the rear wheels of her son's car, and she awoke with the feeling that he shouldn't be driving it. He was about to take a long driving trip, one that she disapproved of. Was the dream a genuine psychic message, or a reflection of her feelings about the trip? Because Leah knew the language of her dreams, she recognized her personal psychic hallmarks in this one. She took it as a warning to pass on to her son. The car seemed to be in good condition, but a closer inspection revealed that one of the rear wheels was in danger of falling off. If it had done so on the highway, Leah's son may have been killed or seriously injured, or stranded in a remote location.

Be extremely careful about warnings. Not every dream of a plane crash means a plane is going to crash, for example. If you misinterpret your information, you can cause a great deal of emotional stress.

Speak gently

If you do offer your psychic insights, do so in a soft and agreeable manner that is easy for another person to accept. Avoid dictatorial statements such as "You must..." "You have to..." Rather, say "I feel that" or "My impression is that it would be best to..." Do not boast that you are infallible or always right. Remember that psychic power sees behind the surface into delicate areas and picks up on the probable outcomes of forces in motion. Forces can change, and so can outcomes.

Decline challenges and requests to perform

Every now and then you will meet someone who thinks it would be loads of laughs for you to perform like a circus act. Perhaps they have an idle curiosity to satisfy. They insist that you demonstrate your talent on the spot. "Can you read my aura right now?" "Should I sell such-and-such a stock?" "What did I eat for lunch last Tuesday?" "What's the winning lottery number?" Treating these flippant requests seriously will only drain your energy and invite more of the same.

Deflect them with something like, "I don't think this is the appropriate place/time/forum for that..." or "Sorry, I'm off duty now." It serves no useful purpose, to you, your gift or to anyone present, to jump because someone insists on it.

Once during the intermission of a lecture, a young man said to me, "What am I thinking right now?" I replied with a smile, "You're wondering whether or not I can tell what you're thinking," and I changed the subject. If you offer psychic consultations on a professional basis, you can say, "If you're interested in a consultation, I'd be happy to discuss how I work and perhaps set up an appointment."

Occasionally you will run into an out-and-out skeptic, who is likely to be hostile as well, who will demand a demonstration to prove you have an ability. Nothing will make a skeptic happy, and anything you offer will be used as more grist for grinding you down.

Decline health matters

Without a medical license, it is against the law to make medical diagnoses. Do not do so. Period. There is a growing profession of medical intuitives who train under a doctor's supervision to act as consultants in medical matters. If using your ability in the health care professions appeals to you, investigate this type of training. There also are many training programs in energy healing, though these still do not qualify you to make medical diagnoses.

Above all, *never* predict if or when somebody—or even a pet—is going to die. You could create a nightmare for that person and others. The time of death is between each soul and the Creator. Forces in motion change moment to moment. No matter what you might sense at any given time, you may not be seeing the whole picture.

Once a psychic, whom I was consulting for a reading, volunteered out of the blue, and rather matter-of-factly, that one of my beloved dogs was soon to die, probably from being hit by a car. I was in a terrible state of anxiety for months. Nothing happened. The dog lived for another ten years and died of old age. Such a reading lacked both responsibility and consideration.

Readings and consultations

Many people who develop their psychic ability give readings and consultations on a professional basis, charging fees for their services. If you wish to become a reader, pay special attention to the foregoing etiquette.

When people seek out a reading, they look upon the reader as an authority. Negative comments and pronouncements can have a devastating effect. This does not mean that a reader should paint a false, rosy picture. Just be sensitive to how things are worded.

Most people get readings because they have problems they wish to solve. A reading should be constructive and empowering. It is not a substitute for professional counseling or therapy. Remind your clients of this.

It is a good idea to make a statement at the beginning of a session that sets out the parameters of the reading. I tell people that the purpose of a reading is to provide insight that will help them make their own decisions. I stress that any impressions of future outcomes are based on forces in motion, and can change as people change their intent and actions. We have free will.

Readings have been outlawed in many places in the past, and even today laws can vary considerably. In the U.S., for example, some states allow readings only for "entertainment purposes," and this purpose must clearly be stated by the practitioners. Familiarize yourself with your local laws.

There are always going to be some people who want readers to tell them what they should do about everything, big and small, going on in their life. I don't encourage dependency on readings.

If you give readings, you will find that some go very well and others are a struggle. We tune into people differently. You might find that your own psychic power will guide you in this matter. When someone asks for a reading, you will know whether or not you should give one. You may not be the right person for them; or, they may want you to tell them something that you really can't guarantee. There is nothing wrong with declining a reading. Gently, of course.

If you have a genuine desire to help people, and you ask your Higher Self to guide you accordingly, you are likely to be a successful reader.

About the Author

Rosemary Ellen Guiley is a leading expert in the metaphysical and paranormal fields. She is the author of more than 60 books on a wide range of topics, including intuition and psychic ability, working with angels and spirits guides, miracle mind consciousness, and spiritual and psychic dreams.

Rosemary also works as a dreamwork facilitator for individuals and groups, and is a Dream Oracle dream interpreter on the DreamSocial.co website. She is a certified hypnotist and conducts regressions for past lives. She is a Tarot reader, and teaches the Tarot and psychic skills. In addition, she researches the afterlife, and investigates cases of paranormal activity and entity interferences and attachments.

Rosemary serves on the board of advisors for the Foundation for Research into Extraterrestrial Encounters, and is a former member of the board of directors of the International Association for the Study of Dreams. She lectures and teaches internationally on a wide range of subjects, is featured frequently in the media, including *Coast to Coast AM* with George Noory; and runs her own publishing company. She lives in Connecticut. Her website is www.visionaryliving.com.

Bibliography and Recommended Reading

Adams, Scott. *The Dilbert Future: Thriving on Business Stupidity in the 21st Century.* New York: HarperBusiness, 1998.

Adrienne, Carol. *The Purpose of Your Life.* New York: William Morrow & Company, 1998.

Artress, Lauren. *Walking A Sacred Path: Rediscovering the Labyrinth as a Sacred Tool.* New York: Riverheard Books, 1995.

Beasley, Victor R. *Psychic power By Design: Applying Your Intuitive Intelligence for Personal and Business Decision-Making.* Livermore, CA: Oughten House Publications, 1995.

Belitz, Charlene and Meg Lundstrom. *The Power of Flow: Practical Ways to Transform Your Life with Meaningful Coincidence.* New York: Harmony Books, 1997.

Borysenko, Joan and Miroslav Borysenko. *The Power of the Mind to Heal.* Carson, CA: Hay House, 1994.

Briggs, John. *Fire in the Crucible: The Alchemy of Creative Genius.* New York: St. Martin's Press, 1988.

Campbell, Don. *The Mozart Effect.* New York: Avon Books, 1997.

Choquette, Sonia. *Your Heart's Desire: Instructions for Creating the Life You Really Want.* New York: Three Rivers Press, 1997.

_____. *Tune In: Let Your Intuition Guide You to Fulfillment and Flow.* Carlsbad, CA: Hay House, 2013.

Csikszentmihalyi, Mihaly. *Flow: The Psychology of Optimal Experience.* New York: HarperCollins, 1990.

Dean, Douglas and John Mihalasky and Sheila Ostrander and Lynn Schroeder. *Executive ESP.* Englewood Cliffs, NJ: Prentice Hall, 1974.

Dossey, Larry. *Healing Words: The Power of Prayer and the Practice of Medicine.* San Francisco: HarperSanFranciso, 1993.

Dyer, Wayne W. *Real Magic: Creating Miracles in Every Day Life.* New York: HarperCollins, 1992.

Einstein, Patricia. *Psychic power: Path to Inner Wisdom.* Rockport, MA: Element Books, 1997.

Emery, Marcia. *Psychic Power Workbook: An Expert's Guide to Unlocking the Wisdom of Your Subconscious Mind.* Englewood Cliffs, NJ: Prentice Hall, 1994.

Gawain, Shakti. *Creative Visualization.* New York: Bantam Books, 1982.

Guiley, Rosemary Ellen. *Harper's Encyclopedia of Mystical and Paranormal Phenomena.* San Francisco: HarperSanFranciso, 1991.

_____. *Calling Upon Angels: How Angels Help Us in Daily Life.* New Milford, CT: Visionary Living, Inc., 2015.

_____. *Dreamwork for Visionary Living.* New Milford, CT: Visionary Living, Inc., 2014.

Harman, Willis and Howard Rheingold. *Higher Creativity: Liberating the Unconscious for Breakthrough Insights.* Los Angeles: Jeremy P. Tarcher, 1984.

Harman, Willis. *Global Mind Change.* Sausalito, CA: Institute of Noetic Sciences, 1998.

Leonard, George and Michael Murphy. *The Life We Are Given.* New York: Jeremy P Tarcher/Putnam, 1995.

Levoy, Gregg. *Callings: Finding and Following an Authentic Life.* New York: Harmony Books, 1997.

Miller, Carolyn. *Creating Miracles: Understanding the Experience of Divine Intervention.* Tiburon, CA: HJ Kramer, 1995.

Mishlove, Jeffrey. T*he Roots of Consciousness* (rev.). Tulsa: Council Oak Books,

Moody, Raymond. *Reunions: Visionary Encounters With Departed Loved Ones.* New York: Villard Books, 1993.

Murphy, Michael and Rhea A White. *In the Zone: Transcendent Experience in Sports.* New York: Penguin Books, 1995.

Naparstek, Belleruth. *Your Sixth Sense: Activating Your Psychic Potential.* San Francisco: HarperSanFrancisco, 1997.

Northrup, Christiane. *Women's Bodies, Women's Wisdom.* New York: Bantam Books, 1994.

Ornstein, Robert. *The Evolution of Consciousness.* New York: Prentice Hall Press, 1991.

Palmer, Helen (ed.). *Inner Knowing.* New York: Jeremy P Tarcher/Putnam, 1998.

Peale, Norman Vincent Peale. *The Power of Positive Thinking.* New York: Prentice Hall, 1952.

Peirce, Penney. *The Intuitive Way: A Guide to Living from Inner Wisdom.* Hillsboro, OR: Beyond Words Publishing, 1997.

_____. *Leap of Perception: The Transforming Power of Your Attention*. New York: Atria Books, 2013.

Radin, Dean I. *The Conscious Universe: The Scientific Truth of Psychic Phenomena*. San Francisco: HarperEdge, 1997.

Remele, Patricia. *Money Freedom: Finding Your Source of Wealth*. Virginia Beach, VA: ARE Press, 1995.

Rosanoff, Nancy. *Psychic power Workout: A Practical Guide to Discovering and Developing Your Inner Knowing*. Boulder Creek, CA: Aslan Publishing, 1988.

Russell, Peter. *Waking Up in Time: Finding Inner Peace in Times of Accelerating Change*. Novato, CA: Origin Press, 1998.

Satprem. *Sri Aurobindo or the Adventure of Consciousness*. Mt. Vernon, WA: Institute for Evolutionary Research, 1993.

Schulz, Mona Lisa. *Awakening Psychic power: Using Your Mind-Body Network for Insight and Healing*. New York: Harmony Books, 1998.

Seale, Alan. *On Becoming a 21st-Century Mystic: Pathways to Intuitive Living*. New York: Skytop Publishing, 1997.

Sherman, Harold. *How to Make ESP Work for You*. Los Angeles: DeVorss & Company, 1964.

Spangler, David. *Every Day Miracles: The Inner Art of Manifestation*. New York: Bantam Books, 1996.

Steiner, Rudolph. *How to Know Higher Worlds*. Hudson, NY: Anthroposophic Press, 1994.

Suzuki, Shunryu. *Zen Mind, Beginner's Mind*. New York: Weatherhill, 1970.

Tenshin, Okakura. *The Book of Tea.* Tokyo: Kodansha International, 1998.

Underhill, Evelyn. *Mysticism.* New York: New American Library, 1974.

Vaughn, Frances E. *Awakening Psychic power.* Garden City, NY: Anchor Books, 1979.

Weil, Andrew. *Spontaneous Healing.* New York: Alfred A. Knopf, 1995.

www.ingramcontent.com/pod-product-compliance
Lightning Source LLC
Chambersburg PA
CBHW020646300426
44112CB00007B/260